Learning Adventism Before Learning Christ

Performance, Hiddenness, and the Search for Truthful Christianity

Michael A. Reahl

Learning Adventism Before Learning Christ
Performance, Hiddenness, and the Search for Truthful Christianity

Published by
Advent Awareness Media & Publishing
Alaska, USA

First Edition, 2026

Cover design by Michael A. Reahl

Printed in the United States of America

Dedication

For those who learned how to hide before they learned how to rest.

For the children who smiled in church while carrying chaos at home.

For the ones who checked their clothes for the smell of smoke before walking into school or Sabbath service.

For those who learned performance before surrender, religion before relationship, and camouflage before truth.

For the exhausted Christians quietly carrying burdens they were never meant to carry.

And for the people still wondering whether Jesus is truly different from the systems that wounded them.

<u>He is.</u>

Author's Note

This book was not written by someone standing comfortably inside a church office.

It was written by someone who spent much of life outside the walls trying to understand why Jesus often felt different from the religious systems surrounding Him.

I grew up inside Seventh-day Adventist Church culture. I attended Adventist schools. I sat through theology classes, prophecy seminars, weeks of prayer, Sabbath services, and countless conversations about truth, standards, doctrine, and identity. And strangely, for a long time, I avoided formal theological training even while deeply loving theology itself.

Part of me believed I could be of more use outside official church structures than within them.

Not because I rejected the church.
Not because I stopped believing truth mattered.
But because I kept finding wounded people far outside the buildings.

People drowning in addiction.
Trauma.
Fear.
Loneliness.
Violence.
Shame.
Exhaustion.

And many of them were deeply afraid of Christians.

Not always of Christ.

Of Christians.

Over the years, my life moved through places I never expected:

military service,

emergency medicine,

law enforcement,

rural Alaska,

human suffering,

crisis scenes,

violence,

death notifications,

drunkenness,

broken homes,

and countless moments where people no longer possessed the strength to pretend they were fine.

Rural Alaska changed how I saw people. In many villages, suffering is harder to camouflage. Addiction becomes visible. Loneliness becomes visible. Grief becomes visible. There are no polished suburban facades hiding reality. Sometimes there are no distractions left at all. Just silence, isolation, exhaustion, survival, and human beings trying to make it through another day. Ironically, some of the most spiritually honest conversations I have ever had happened in places where people no longer possessed the energy to maintain religious appearances. In many ways, those experiences forced me to confront how much of Christianity can quietly become performance while people suffer directly beside us.

Ironically, some of the most spiritually honest people I ever met were nowhere near church culture.

Eventually I completed theological studies, an M.Div., and now doctoral work. But even now, I still often feel more like an evangelist standing outside institutional walls than safely inside them. I remain deeply convinced theology matters. Doctrine matters. Truth matters. The Sabbath matters. The gospel matters.

But I have also become convinced that many people learned religion before they learned rest in Christ.

Many learned how to perform before they learned how to surrender.
Many learned camouflage before confession.
Many learned Adventism before they learned Jesus relationally.

Readers may notice the unusual placement of Chapter Six.Five, "The Strong Child." The numbering is intentional. Throughout this book, I explore themes of hiddenness, fragmentation, survival, and the parts of ourselves that exist quietly beneath performance and religious identity. The "half chapter" reflects that reality. It represents the unfinished spaces many people carry internally, the interrupted formation beneath outward strength, and the hidden survival patterns that often exist between religious systems and self-righteousness. In many ways, the strong child exists between the border guard and the Pharisee.

This book is not an attack against the church that raised me. It is not written from bitterness, rebellion, or theological compromise. In many ways, it is written from grief.

Grief over how easy it is for human beings to hide.
Grief over how often religious performance replaces truthful discipleship.
Grief over how many exhausted Christians quietly carry burdens Jesus never asked them to carry.
Grief over how many wounded people are afraid to approach believers who claim to represent Christ.

But beneath that grief is still hope.

Because I believe Jesus is still different.

Different from performance driven religion.

Different from camouflage Christianity.

Different from systems that reward appearances while ignoring hidden pain.

The Jesus I encounter in Scripture moves toward broken people instead of away from them. He tells the truth without cruelty. He exposes sin without abandoning sinners. He invites exhausted people into rest instead of deeper performance.

That is the burden behind these pages.

Not to tear down faith.

But to plead for truthful Christianity again.

A Christianity where people no longer need to pretend.

Where confession exists.

Where grace is real.

Where holiness remains relational.

Where theology leads people toward Christ instead of merely toward systems.

Where wounded people can encounter believers who actually resemble Jesus.

I am still learning to live that myself.

Table of Contents

Introduction: Learning to Hide

I do not remember exactly when I first learned to hide.

I only know that by the time I was young, it already felt normal.

Some children grow up learning safety, stability, and confidence. Others grow up learning concealment. They learn how to read tension before words are spoken. They learn how to recognize instability by the smell of cigarette smoke on clothes, by the silence after arguments, or by the feeling that home could shift emotionally at any moment. They learn how to smile in public while quietly carrying fear, shame, confusion, or embarrassment underneath.

I learned how to survive long before I understood theology.

Like many children raised around addiction, instability, and hidden pain, I developed two versions of myself. One version existed publicly. That version smiled at church, acted normal, and tried to fit into the world around me. The other version carried anxiety, confusion, fear, and the constant awareness that life at home did not look like the polished Christian lives surrounding me.

Over time, I became skilled at hiding.

I learned how to pretend I was fine.
I learned how to hide embarrassment.
I learned how to avoid exposure.
I learned how to survive.

And honestly, church complicated that tension.

Not because faith itself was false. Not because doctrine was meaningless. But because I slowly began realizing there is a difference between learning Christ and learning how to survive religious culture. There is a difference between transformation and performance. There is a difference between truthful Christianity and camouflage Christianity.

I learned how to behave like an Adventist before I learned how to rest honestly in Jesus.

I learned standards before surrender.
Performance before transparency.
Appearance before confession.
Rules before relationship.

As I grew older, I started noticing something deeply unsettling. Many people around me seemed spiritually polished but emotionally hidden. Families quietly concealed addiction, anger, financial struggle, abuse, pornography, loneliness, depression, and exhaustion while maintaining outward religious appearance. We knew how to look stable. We knew how to sound spiritual. We knew how to defend truth. But many of us did not know how to be truthful.

The church often became a place where people learned how to hide better.

That realization disturbed me because Jesus seemed entirely different from the religious culture surrounding Him. Christ continually moved toward exposed people. He sat with sinners, defended the ashamed, restored failures, touched lepers, confronted hypocrisy, and welcomed broken people who no longer possessed the strength to maintain appearances.

The people most comfortable around Jesus were often the people least comfortable inside religious performance systems.

Then one day I heard a simple story that unsettled me deeply.

A customs officer watched a man cross the border every day carrying bags of sand on a bicycle. Suspicious that something illegal was occurring, the officer repeatedly searched the bags, sifted through the sand, and examined every detail carefully. Years later, after retirement, the officer finally discovered the truth.

The man had been smuggling bicycles the entire time.

That story stayed with me because I realized how often religion works the same way.

We become obsessed with inspecting the sand:

behavior,

appearance,

rules,

metrics,

systems,

prophecy charts,

dietary standards,

religious culture,

institutional loyalty,

and external performance.

Meanwhile, we quietly miss the obvious Christ standing directly in front of us.

This book is not an attack against Seventh-day Adventist Church. It is not an argument against doctrine, holiness, obedience, or biblical truth. I still believe truth matters. I still believe theology matters. I still believe the law of God matters.

But I have become convinced that many people learn religion before they learn surrender. Many inherit church culture before encountering Jesus personally. Many become fluent in religious performance while remaining spiritually exhausted, emotionally hidden, and terrified of being truly known.

In many ways, this book is about hiddenness.

It is about survival becoming identity.

It is about shame becoming performance.

It is about religious systems becoming camouflage.

It is about people learning how to appear transformed while quietly remaining afraid.

But more than that, this book is about Christ.

Not merely doctrinal correctness about Him.

Not merely institutional loyalty to Him.

Not merely behavioral conformity in His name.

Christ Himself.

The Jesus who was never afraid of the smell of smoke.
The Jesus who moved toward broken people instead of away from them.
The Jesus who exposed false religion while offering rest to exhausted sinners.
The Jesus who invited people into truth instead of performance.
The Jesus who said:

"Come to me, all who labor and are heavy laden, and I will give you rest" (Matt. 11:28, ESV).

I believe many Christians today are exhausted because they have spent years trying to maintain appearances rather than abiding honestly in Christ. They have become experts at sifting sand while quietly overlooking the bicycle standing directly before them.

This book is a plea to stop hiding long enough to encounter Jesus truthfully.

Because I have become convinced that many of us learned Adventism before we ever truly learned Christ.

And those are not always the same thing.

PART ONE:
LEARNING TO HIDE

Chapter One:
The Smell of Smoke

Some people hear the word "childhood" and think of safety.

I usually think about survival.

Not dramatic survival in the movie sense. Quiet survival. The kind where you learn how to read rooms before you learn algebra. The kind where you can feel tension before anybody speaks. The kind where your body stays alert even during normal moments because instability never fully announces itself before arriving.

I do not remember exactly when I became aware that my life was different from other people's lives. I only know that eventually I began noticing things other kids did not seem worried about.

The smell of cigarette smoke on clothes.
Whether people would notice.
Whether teachers could tell.
Whether church members silently judged.
Whether I looked poor.
Whether I looked unstable.
Whether I looked normal enough.

Children learn quickly what brings embarrassment.

I remember checking my clothes before being around other people. I remember trying to make sure I smelled acceptable before school or church. I remember understanding very early that certain smells communicated things about your life that you could not control. Smoke meant instability. Smoke meant dysfunction. Smoke meant people might quietly categorize you before you ever spoke.

So I learned concealment.

I learned how to present a cleaner version of reality publicly than what existed privately. And honestly, I became good at it.

That skill followed me into church culture naturally because many churches already function through appearance management whether they realize it or not. People know how to smile at the right moments. Families know how to present stability publicly while hiding collapse privately. Everyone understands the silent rules even when nobody says them out loud.

Certain struggles are acceptable.
Others are dangerous.

The dangerous struggles are the ones that threaten image.

That creates an environment where many people never learn honesty. They learn performance instead.

Looking back now, I realize I learned survival long before I learned surrender. I learned how to behave correctly before I understood grace. I learned how to appear spiritually functional before I knew what it meant to abide honestly in Christ.

And honestly, I think many people in church are doing the same thing.

Some people hide addiction.
Some hide pornography.
Some hide depression.
Some hide resentment.
Some hide exhaustion.
Some hide loneliness.

Some hide trauma.

Some hide fear.

But everyone becomes very skilled at pretending.

The strange thing is that Jesus never seemed impressed by pretending.

Throughout the Gospels, the people most drawn toward Christ were usually people who had already lost the ability to maintain appearances. Prostitutes, tax collectors, lepers, demoniacs, and publicly broken sinners constantly moved toward Him because Jesus created something religious culture often failed to create: safety for truthful people.

Religious leaders hated this about Him.

In Luke 7, Jesus entered the house of Simon the Pharisee where a sinful woman approached Him publicly weeping. She cried at His feet, wiped them with her hair, and poured ointment on Him while everyone in the room silently judged her existence.

Simon immediately thought:

"If this man were a prophet, he would have known who and what sort of woman this is who is touching him, for she is a sinner" (Luke 7:39, ESV).

That verse says more about Simon than the woman.

Simon interpreted holiness through distance from contaminated people. He believed righteousness required separation from visibly broken humanity. The woman represented shame. Reputation. Failure. Public exposure.

But Jesus did not recoil from her.

That matters deeply to me.

Because many of us grew up believing God reacts like religious people react. We assume He backs away from weakness. We assume He distances Himself from addiction, instability, trauma, shame, or visible failure.

But Jesus repeatedly moved toward those exact people.

The Pharisees often asked:
"How close can holiness get to broken people before becoming contaminated?"

Jesus demonstrated:
"How close can grace get to broken people before they are transformed?"

That difference changes everything.

One of the reasons I struggle with shallow Christian clichés is because they often feel disconnected from real suffering. When someone grows up around instability, addiction, fear, or emotional chaos, polished religious language can feel artificial very quickly. People say things like:
"Just trust God."
"Everything happens for a reason."
"God is in control."

And while some of those statements contain truth, they can also become ways of avoiding uncomfortable reality. They become spiritual shortcuts around honest pain.

Jesus never seemed interested in shortcuts around pain.

He entered it.

He touched lepers.
He wept publicly.
He sat with sinners.
He defended ashamed people.

He restored failures.

He moved toward wounded humanity instead of away from it.

That is one reason Jesus felt different from much of the religious culture surrounding Him.

He did not seem afraid of broken people.

Honestly, sometimes church people seemed more uncomfortable around visibly hurting individuals than Jesus ever was.

That realization slowly began reshaping how I understood theology itself. Theology was no longer merely about correct information regarding God. Theology became deeply connected to the character of Christ. What is God actually like? How does He respond to brokenness? What does holiness really mean?

Because if holiness merely creates distance from struggling people, then the Pharisees were holy.

But Jesus revealed a different kind of holiness entirely.

A holiness strong enough to enter contaminated places without becoming contaminated Himself.
A holiness rooted in compassion rather than superiority.
A holiness that exposed sin while still moving toward sinners.

That distinction matters because many believers secretly live terrified of being fully known. They fear that if people discovered the truth about their struggles, thoughts, background, family history, addiction, or weakness, they would lose belonging.

So they continue hiding.

Some hide behind success.

Some hide behind ministry.

Some hide behind theology.

Some hide behind religious performance.

But eventually hiding becomes exhausting.

David understood this deeply after concealing his own sin:

"For when I kept silent, my bones wasted away through my groaning all day long" (Ps. 32:3, ESV).

Concealment always costs something.

The soul was never designed to survive indefinitely behind camouflage.

That is why truthful Christianity matters so deeply to me now. Not performative Christianity. Not image centered Christianity. Truthful Christianity.

Christianity where confession exists.

Christianity where weakness can be acknowledged.

Christianity where grace is larger than appearances.

Christianity where people no longer need to pretend they are already healed in order to belong.

Because I think many believers are exhausted from carrying identities they were never meant to sustain.

And maybe that exhaustion explains why Jesus' invitation still feels so radical:

"Come to me, all who labor and are heavy laden, and I will give you rest" (Matt. 11:28, ESV).

Not:

"Come perform."

Not:

"Come impress."

Not:

"Come hide better."

Come to Me.

Honestly.

Openly.

Truthfully.

For many people, that may be the hardest thing they have ever done.

Chapter Two
The Book Fair

I still remember the feeling of standing in the hallway during the school book fair pretending I did not care.

Other kids walked around excited, holding colorful books, posters, pencils, and little trinkets they had convinced their parents to buy for them. Some of them laughed while comparing what they got. Others flipped through shiny pages while talking about which books they wanted next.

I remember acting uninterested.

That is what kids do when they are embarrassed.

You pretend something does not matter when you already know you cannot have it.

I knew there was no money for books. Sometimes there was barely money for food. But children become skilled actors very quickly. You learn how to smile casually. You learn how to shrug your shoulders like you chose not to participate. You learn how to protect yourself from humiliation before anybody notices the truth.

So I stood there pretending.

I remember staring at the spinning book rack long enough to look occupied while trying not to make eye contact with anyone holding something they were excited about.

Looking back now, I realize that hallway taught me something dangerous: how to hide need.

Not solve need.

Hide it.

That lesson followed me into adulthood and eventually into church culture because many churches unintentionally reward the appearance of strength more than the honesty of weakness.

The hallway changed, but the instinct remained the same.

People learn quickly what kinds of struggles are acceptable publicly. You can talk about being "busy." You can admit you are "stressed." Sometimes you can even acknowledge past struggles as long as they are resolved neatly enough.

But active weakness?

Current addiction?

Ongoing shame?

Fear?

Depression?

Doubt?

Exhaustion?

Spiritual numbness?

Those things become dangerous.

So people do exactly what children do at book fairs:
they pretend they do not need anything.

And honestly, I think a lot of Christians are starving while trying to look full.

That realization began bothering me deeply as I got older. I started noticing how much energy religious communities spend maintaining appearances. Entire congregations quietly learn how to present polished versions of themselves while avoiding truthful vulnerability.

The strange thing is that Scripture constantly moves in the opposite direction.

Jesus repeatedly moved toward people who openly knew they were desperate.

Blind beggars cried publicly.
Demoniacs screamed publicly.
The sinful woman wept publicly.
Tax collectors repented publicly.
The lepers openly displayed contamination nobody else wanted near them.

Yet those were often the people closest to Christ emotionally.

The Pharisees, meanwhile, remained obsessed with appearance.

In Matthew 23, Jesus exposed this directly:

"Woe to you, scribes and Pharisees, hypocrites! For you clean the outside of the cup and the plate, but inside they are full of greed and self-indulgence" (Matt. 23:25, ESV).

That verse haunted me once I started truly seeing church culture differently.

Because Jesus was not criticizing obvious sinners there.
He was criticizing polished religion.

People who looked spiritually successful externally while remaining internally unhealthy.

That is terrifying because it means religious activity can become camouflage. Church attendance can become camouflage. Ministry involvement can become camouflage. Theology itself can become camouflage.

A person can know doctrine thoroughly while remaining emotionally hidden and spiritually exhausted.

And honestly, I think many of us learned exactly how to do that.

We learned how to sound transformed before we learned how to be truthful.
We learned how to perform stability before we learned surrender.
We learned how to defend theology before we learned how to rest in grace.

I think that is one reason Jesus often seemed harder on religious leaders than openly broken people.

Open sinners usually knew they were needy.
Religious performers often believed they were healthy.

In Luke 18, Jesus tells the story of a Pharisee and a tax collector praying in the temple. The Pharisee publicly thanks God that he is morally superior to other people while listing his religious accomplishments. Meanwhile the tax collector stands at a distance unable even to lift his eyes toward heaven:

"God, be merciful to me, a sinner!" (Luke 18:13, ESV).

Then Jesus says something shocking:

"This man went down to his house justified, rather than the other" (Luke 18:14, ESV).

Why?

Because honesty opened the door to grace.

The Pharisee had religion.
The tax collector had truth.

That distinction matters more than many churches realize.

As I grew older, I began noticing that many believers carried deep fear regarding exposure. Not just fear of sin being exposed, but fear of weakness itself being visible. People feared appearing unstable, needy, emotionally struggling, financially broken, spiritually confused, or imperfect.

So everyone learned presentation management.

Families hid dysfunction.
Pastors hid burnout.
Men hid addiction.
Teenagers hid depression.
Churches hid conflict.
Everyone kept smiling.

And slowly I began wondering:
What if much of what we call "Christian maturity" is actually just polished concealment?

That question disturbed me because I genuinely loved theology. I loved Scripture. I loved studying doctrine. I still do. But I also realized theology can either reveal Christ or become another hiding place.

The Pharisees knew theology extremely well.

Jesus even acknowledged their doctrinal position at times. Yet somehow they could study Scripture constantly while missing the Messiah standing directly in front of them.

Jesus said:

"You search the Scriptures because you think that in them you have eternal life; and it is they that bear witness about me" (John 5:39, ESV).

That may be one of the most frightening verses in the Bible for religious people.

It means someone can become obsessed with religious study while quietly missing Christ Himself.

Like the border guard searching sand while bicycles rolled past in plain sight.

I think that happens more often than we realize.

People debate prophetic timelines while ignoring hurting people beside them.

People defend standards while neglecting mercy.

People obsess over behavior while avoiding confession.

People preserve systems while forgetting why those systems existed originally.

Even the Sabbath can become this way.

The Sabbath was meant to reveal rest in God, dependence upon Him, and trust in His provision. Yet many people experience Sabbath primarily through anxiety:

Did I do enough?

Did I break the rules?

Was this allowed?

Was that sinful?

The day meant to teach rest quietly becomes another performance test.

That is why Jesus said:

"The Sabbath was made for man, not man for the Sabbath" (Mark 2:27, ESV).

Christ constantly redirected people back toward the heart of God rather than mere behavioral compliance.

Not because obedience does not matter.

But because obedience detached from relationship becomes exhausting.

I think many believers are tired because they are carrying forms of Christianity built more around appearance than abiding.

And maybe that is why so many people secretly feel alone in church.

Because performance isolates.

If everyone must appear strong, nobody can be known honestly.
If nobody can be known honestly, then nobody can truly rest.

The book fair hallway taught me how to hide need.

Jesus is still teaching me how to bring need into the light instead.

Chapter Three:
Camouflage Christianity

One of the strangest things about camouflage is that its entire purpose is to make something disappear while it is still technically present.

The object exists.

The person exists.

But the real thing becomes hidden beneath carefully designed patterns meant to blend into the environment.

I understand camouflage well.

The military teaches camouflage intentionally. Law enforcement uses it operationally. Hunters use it strategically. The purpose is survival, concealment, protection, and reduced exposure.

But long before I understood camouflage professionally, I had already learned it emotionally.

I learned how to blend into environments without exposing too much of myself. I learned how to monitor reactions carefully. I learned how to present the version of myself most likely to remain accepted in whatever room I entered.

Church culture sometimes strengthened those instincts instead of healing them.

Because if we are honest, many religious environments quietly reward camouflage Christianity.

People learn how to:

- sound spiritually mature,

- quote the right verses,

- use the right language,

- avoid the wrong behaviors publicly,

- and maintain respectable appearances,

while remaining deeply unknown underneath.

The frightening thing is that eventually even the person wearing the camouflage can forget who they really are beneath it.

That is what performative religion often does. It slowly disconnects people from truthful self-awareness. Instead of honestly bringing weakness before God, people begin managing perception constantly. Spiritual life becomes more about maintaining the image than nurturing the soul.

Jesus confronted this repeatedly.

In Matthew 23, Christ described the Pharisees as:

"Whitewashed tombs, which outwardly appear beautiful, but within are full of dead people's bones and all uncleanness" (Matt. 23:27, ESV).

That image is brutal.

A whitewashed tomb looks clean externally. From a distance it appears respectable, polished, and spiritually impressive. But beneath the surface sits death hidden under paint.

The terrifying thing is that Jesus was describing deeply religious people.

People who attended services.
People who studied Scripture.
People who defended doctrine.
People who believed themselves spiritually serious.

Yet somehow their religion had become camouflage instead of transformation.

That possibility unsettles me deeply because I think many Christians quietly live this way without realizing it.

We become experts at presenting the "acceptable Christian self."
The calm self.
The stable self.
The disciplined self.
The polished self.

Meanwhile the real self remains exhausted, ashamed, afraid, addicted, lonely, angry, confused, or emotionally numb underneath.

And because everyone around us is often doing the same thing, the camouflage becomes normalized.

Church becomes a room full of hidden people complimenting each other's disguises.

That sounds harsh, but honestly I think many believers already feel this internally even if they have never said it aloud.

The strange thing is that Jesus consistently disrupted camouflage.

He asked questions people were trying to avoid.
He exposed hidden motives.
He confronted religious performance.
He brought concealed realities into the light.

But He did not expose people merely to humiliate them.
He exposed people so healing could begin.

That distinction matters.

Many people fear exposure because they associate exposure with condemnation. They assume if God truly saw them fully, He would withdraw from them the same way people often do.

But Scripture repeatedly reveals the opposite.

In John 4, Jesus met the Samaritan woman at the well and began exposing details about her life:

"You have had five husbands, and the one you now have is not your husband" (John 4:18, ESV).

What amazes me is that she did not run away.

Why?

Because Jesus exposed her without humiliating her.

That is incredibly important.

Religious performance usually says:
"Hide your brokenness until you become acceptable."

Jesus says:
"Bring your brokenness into the light so transformation can begin."

Those are radically different systems.

One produces camouflage.
The other produces freedom.

I think many Christians secretly live exhausted because camouflage requires enormous emotional energy. Pretending is tiring. Monitoring appearances constantly is tiring. Trying to maintain spiritual image while carrying hidden struggles is exhausting.

David described this internal collapse after hiding sin:

"For when I kept silent, my bones wasted away through my groaning all day long" (Ps. 32:3, ESV).

Concealment slowly destroys people internally.

And honestly, many churches unknowingly participate in this destruction by creating environments where weakness feels unsafe. People begin believing they must arrive already healed in order to belong. So they hide the very struggles Christ wants to redeem.

The irony is painful.

The church was supposed to become a refuge for sinners.
Instead many people experience it as a stage for performers.

I think this is one reason Jesus often seemed emotionally safer than religious systems built in His name.

Broken people constantly moved toward Jesus.
Meanwhile religious leaders frequently moved away from broken people.

That should disturb us.

Because if sinners felt safer around Christ than around religious communities, then something about our communities may not reflect His character fully.

This realization forced me to rethink holiness entirely.

Growing up, holiness sometimes felt like distance from contaminated people or contaminated environments. The holier someone appeared, the more separated they often seemed from visible weakness.

But Jesus demonstrated a different kind of holiness altogether.

He touched lepers.

He ate with tax collectors.

He defended adulterers from public destruction.

He allowed sinful people near Him.

He entered contaminated environments constantly.

And somehow His holiness remained intact.

That means holiness is not fragility.

Jesus did not become sinful because He moved toward broken people. Instead, His presence transformed the environments He entered. His holiness was restorative rather than performative.

That changed how I began understanding theology itself.

Theology is not merely about having correct information regarding God. Theology is ultimately about knowing His character accurately. And if our theology makes us less compassionate, less truthful, less humble, or less willing to move toward broken people, then something has gone wrong.

Paul warned about this danger directly:

"Knowledge puffs up, but love builds up" (1 Cor. 8:1, ESV).

A person can become theologically informed while remaining spiritually immature. In fact, theology itself can become camouflage if knowledge replaces surrender.

I think that happens often in religious cultures built heavily around doctrinal precision. People begin equating theological correctness with spiritual maturity. But Jesus consistently revealed that truth without love becomes distortion.

This is why truthful Christianity matters so deeply to me now.

Not shallow authenticity.

Not performative vulnerability.

Not emotional exhibitionism.

Truthfulness.

The ability to stand honestly before God without disguise.

The ability to confess weakness without terror.

The ability to stop managing image constantly.

The ability to let Christ transform the actual person beneath the camouflage.

Because eventually every disguise becomes exhausting.

And maybe that is why Jesus' invitation still feels so radical:

"Come to me, all who labor and are heavy laden, and I will give you rest" (Matt. 11:28, ESV).

Rest is impossible while maintaining camouflage.

Eventually someone has to stop hiding.

PART TWO:
LEARNING ADVENTISM

Chapter Four
Sifting Sand

The older I became, the more I started noticing how easy it is for religious people to become obsessed with details while quietly missing the point.

Not because details are meaningless.

Not because doctrine does not matter.

But because human beings naturally drift toward measurable religion.

Rules feel safer than relationship.

Systems feel safer than surrender.

Performance feels safer than dependence.

You can measure behavior.

You cannot easily measure abiding.

That tension exists inside nearly every religious movement, but I think it becomes especially powerful inside communities with strong doctrinal identity like Seventh-day Adventist Church. Adventism carries enormous theological richness:

- the sanctuary,

- Sabbath,

- prophecy,

- health reform,

- the state of the dead,

- the Three Angels' Messages,

- the cosmic conflict,

- righteousness by faith.

These doctrines matter deeply.

But somewhere along the way, many people quietly learn how to defend the system before they learn how to rest in Christ.

That is where the problem begins.

I started noticing conversations constantly revolving around:

- exact Sabbath timing,

- dietary precision,

- prophetic speculation,

- dress standards,

- church politics,

- institutional loyalty,

- behavioral appearance,

- and theological technicalities.

Meanwhile people sitting directly beside us were drowning emotionally and spiritually.

Marriages were collapsing quietly.
Teenagers were hiding depression.
Men were addicted.
Families were exhausted.
People were lonely.
Some secretly doubted God entirely.
Others hated themselves while pretending to be spiritually mature.

But often we kept discussing sand.

That image kept haunting me because it perfectly describes how religious systems sometimes function.

The border guard spends years inspecting bags of sand while bicycles pass directly in front of him every single day.

And honestly, I think many Christians do the same thing with Jesus.

We inspect secondary things endlessly while quietly overlooking Christ Himself.

The frightening part is that the Pharisees did this while sincerely believing they were defending truth.

That matters.

The Pharisees were not atheists.
They were not pagans.
They were highly disciplined religious men committed to preserving doctrinal faithfulness and moral order. Yet somehow they could memorize Scripture while resisting the Messiah Scripture pointed toward.

Jesus told them:

"You search the Scriptures because you think that in them you have eternal life; and it is they that bear witness about me" (John 5:39, ESV).

That verse unsettles me deeply.

Because it means it is possible to become consumed with religious study while quietly missing Christ Himself.

A person can know theology and still not know Jesus relationally.

That realization changed how I began thinking about church culture entirely.

I started asking myself uncomfortable questions.

What if some people know Adventism better than they know Christ?
What if many believers inherited religious systems before they experienced surrender?
What if churches unintentionally teach image management more effectively than discipleship?
What if some forms of "spiritual maturity" are actually just refined performance?

Those questions disturbed me because I genuinely love theology. I love doctrine. I love studying Scripture. I believe truth matters deeply. But I also realized theology can either reveal Christ or become another hiding place from Him.

That sounds extreme until you read the Gospels carefully.

The Pharisees used theology defensively.
Jesus used theology redemptively.

The Pharisees weaponized truth to reinforce superiority.
Jesus used truth to restore broken people.

The difference is enormous.

One builds religious performers.
The other creates disciples.

I think this becomes especially dangerous when obedience becomes disconnected from relationship. Once obedience loses relational context, Christianity slowly transforms into anxiety management.

People start asking:

Did I keep the rules correctly?

Did I fail spiritually?

Did I measure up?

Was that sinful?

Am I still acceptable to God?

The Christian life becomes exhausting because people are constantly monitoring themselves rather than abiding in Christ.

That is one reason Jesus' words regarding the Sabbath matter so deeply:

"The Sabbath was made for man, not man for the Sabbath" (Mark 2:27, ESV).

The Pharisees had transformed a gift into a burden.

What was meant to reveal trust, rest, and dependence upon God had become another religious checkpoint where people feared failure constantly. Instead of experiencing communion with God, many experienced anxiety regarding behavioral precision.

And honestly, I think that still happens today.

Some believers experience the Sabbath more as pressure than delight.

More as surveillance than sanctuary.

More as fear than rest.

That should concern us because the Sabbath was supposed to reveal the character of God, not obscure Him.

The same thing can happen with every doctrine.

Prophecy without Christ becomes fear.

Health reform without Christ becomes superiority.

Standards without Christ become performance.
The law without Christ becomes exhaustion.

Paul confronted this exact problem in Galatians:

"Are you so foolish? Having begun by the Spirit, are you now being perfected by the flesh?" (Gal. 3:3, ESV).

That verse describes many religious people perfectly.

We begin with grace.
Then we quietly spend the rest of our lives trying to maintain ourselves through performance.

The exhausting result is a culture where many believers constantly feel spiritually inadequate because they are trying to carry a burden Christ never intended them to carry.

Jesus said:

"Come to me, all who labor and are heavy laden, and I will give you rest" (Matt. 11:28, ESV).

But many religious systems unintentionally teach the opposite:
"Come perform."
"Come prove yourself."
"Come maintain appearances."
"Come hide your weakness better."

That is not the gospel.

The gospel begins with surrender, not image management.

And honestly, I think that is why Jesus felt so threatening to the Pharisees. He exposed how much of their spirituality depended upon visibility, status, and public performance. He kept redirecting attention away from religious image and back toward the condition of the heart.

That is why He said:

"This people honors me with their lips, but their heart is far from me" (Matt. 15:8, ESV).

External correctness without relational surrender eventually becomes hollow.

I think many believers sense this internally even if they struggle to articulate it. They feel exhausted trying to maintain spiritual appearance while quietly remaining disconnected from joy, rest, honesty, or intimacy with Christ.

Some know the rules thoroughly but feel emotionally numb.
Some defend doctrine passionately while secretly feeling spiritually empty.
Some attend church faithfully while privately wondering why they still feel so distant from God.

Maybe part of the answer is simpler than we realize.

Maybe we became so focused on sifting sand that we overlooked the bicycle standing directly in front of us the entire time.

Maybe Christianity was never supposed to revolve around mastering religious systems first.

Maybe it was always supposed to begin with Christ Himself.

Chapter Five
The Border Guard

The story sounds almost ridiculous the first time you hear it.

A customs officer notices a man crossing the border every day carrying large bags of sand on a bicycle. Convinced something illegal is happening, the officer searches the bags constantly. He sifts through the sand carefully, checks every detail, and remains certain contraband is hidden somewhere inside.

Nothing is ever found.

Years later, after retirement, the officer finally asks the man what he had been smuggling all along.

The man smiles and answers:
"Bicycles."

The genius of the story is not the smuggling.
It is the blindness.

The obvious thing remained visible the entire time, but the officer became so obsessed with inspecting secondary details that he completely overlooked what was directly in front of him every single day.

That story unsettled me deeply because I realized how often religion functions exactly the same way.

People become consumed with:

- rule precision,

- prophetic timelines,

- theological arguments,

- institutional identity,

- behavioral monitoring,

- doctrinal technicalities,

- and external performance,

while quietly missing Jesus standing in plain sight.

The strange thing is that religious people often feel extremely productive while doing this. The border guard was busy every day. Focused. Disciplined. Serious. He probably felt responsible and morally justified in his work.

But sincerity does not guarantee clarity.

That matters because many religious systems unintentionally reward obsessive focus on visible compliance while neglecting the deeper relational realities underneath. People learn how to monitor behavior carefully while quietly ignoring pride, fear, shame, bitterness, exhaustion, self-righteousness, and lack of compassion.

Jesus confronted this repeatedly.

In Matthew 23, He tells the Pharisees:

"You blind guides, straining out a gnat and swallowing a camel!" (Matt. 23:24, ESV).

That image is almost humorous until you realize how devastating it actually is.

The Pharisees were filtering tiny ceremonial impurities from their drinks while simultaneously ignoring massive spiritual corruption within themselves. They obsessed over microscopic religious details while overlooking enormous relational failures.

They were sifting sand.

And honestly, I think churches still do this constantly.

We debate dietary precision while ignoring loneliness.
We defend standards while neglecting mercy.
We monitor appearances while people quietly collapse emotionally beside us.
We argue theology while marriages fail silently.
We obsess over prophetic speculation while remaining disconnected from compassion.

Sometimes we become so focused on being technically correct that we stop looking like Jesus entirely.

That realization disturbed me deeply because I genuinely believe doctrine matters. Truth matters. Theology matters. But Jesus consistently revealed that truth disconnected from love becomes distortion.

Paul understood this clearly:

"If I... understand all mysteries and all knowledge... but have not love, I am nothing" (1 Cor. 13:2, ESV).

Nothing.

That verse terrifies religious performers because it means theological brilliance can coexist with spiritual emptiness.

A person can defend prophecy flawlessly while remaining harsh, proud, emotionally distant, and spiritually exhausted. A church can maintain doctrinal purity while quietly lacking compassion, humility, honesty, or grace.

The Pharisees prove this painfully.

They knew Scripture.

They defended truth.

They protected religious structure.

They emphasized obedience.

Yet somehow prostitutes and tax collectors recognized Jesus faster than they did.

That should disturb every religious community deeply.

How could visibly broken sinners identify the Messiah more quickly than professional theologians?

I think part of the answer is simple:
broken people usually know they need grace.
Performers often believe they need validation.

That difference changes everything.

Jesus repeatedly moved toward people who no longer possessed functioning disguises. The lepers could not hide contamination. The demoniacs could not maintain appearances. The tax collectors were already socially rejected. The sinful woman in Luke 7 had no reputation left to protect.

But the Pharisees still had images to maintain.

And image management blinds people.

When preserving appearance becomes central, truth becomes threatening instead of liberating. Exposure feels dangerous because identity depends upon perception rather than Christ.

That is why many churches quietly struggle with honesty. People become terrified of vulnerability because vulnerability threatens belonging. Everyone learns how to perform spiritual stability while privately carrying enormous hidden burdens.

The result is often emotionally exhausted Christianity.

People know doctrine but not rest.
People know standards but not surrender.
People know church culture but not intimacy with Christ.

That is exactly what Jesus confronted when He said:

"This people honors me with their lips, but their heart is far from me" (Matt. 15:8, ESV).

Outward religion without inward surrender eventually becomes hollow performance.

I think this becomes especially dangerous inside highly structured religious cultures because structure itself can create the illusion of spiritual health. If someone:

- attends church,

- follows standards,

- speaks correctly,

- participates in ministry,

- and avoids visible scandal,

they may appear spiritually mature externally while remaining deeply disconnected internally.

The camouflage becomes convincing.

Even to themselves.

That may be one of the most frightening realities of all:
people can become so accustomed to performance that they no longer
recognize their own exhaustion.

I think that is why Jesus' invitation still feels radically different from many
religious systems.

He did not say:
"Come impress Me."
"Come prove yourself."
"Come maintain appearances."

He said:

"Come to me, all who labor and are heavy laden, and I will give you rest" (Matt.
11:28, ESV).

Rest.

Not performance.
Not image management.
Not religious anxiety.

Rest.

That invitation matters deeply because many believers are carrying spiritual
burdens Christ never asked them to carry. They spend enormous emotional
energy trying to appear transformed instead of honestly abiding in Him.

The border guard thought the sand was the issue.

Meanwhile bicycles rolled past him every day in plain sight.

I think many Christians are doing the same thing with Jesus.

We become obsessed with secondary things while quietly overlooking the center of Christianity itself:

Christ.

His character.

His grace.

His righteousness.

His presence.

His invitation into truthful surrender.

And honestly, maybe the most dangerous part is that we can spend years doing it while sincerely believing we are protecting the truth.

Chapter Six
The Pharisee in Me

It would be easy to write a book like this pretending the Pharisees were always "other people."

Pastors.

Religious leaders.

Institutional gatekeepers.

Legalistic church members.

But if I am honest, I have to admit something uncomfortable:

I understand the Pharisee more than I want to.

Not because I reject grace.

Not because I hate people.

But because survival and religious performance naturally create Pharisaical instincts inside human beings.

Especially when identity becomes tied to appearing correct.

The Pharisee is not merely a historical figure.

The Pharisee is the part of all of us that wants control, certainty, validation, and visible righteousness.

The Pharisee wants to feel safe by measuring spirituality externally.

The Pharisee wants categories.

The Pharisee wants measurable holiness.

The Pharisee wants assurance through performance.

And honestly, I think many people drift toward Phariseeism not because they are evil, but because they are afraid.

Afraid of chaos.

Afraid of failure.

Afraid of exposure.

Afraid of uncertainty.

Afraid of losing identity.

Performance creates the illusion of control.

That realization hit me slowly over time.

I started noticing how easily I could become internally judgmental while still sounding spiritual externally. I could evaluate people based on behavior, appearances, theological precision, or visible discipline while quietly ignoring the deeper realities of the heart.

I could become more disturbed by visible weakness than hidden pride.

More focused on external order than internal surrender.

More interested in being right than being loving.

That is Phariseeism.

And the terrifying thing is that Phariseeism can wear extremely religious clothing.

The Pharisees prayed.

Studied Scripture.

Fasted.

Defended truth.

Protected morality.

Believed in holiness.

Yet Jesus repeatedly confronted them more harshly than openly broken sinners.

Why?

Because the Pharisees had learned how to hide behind religion itself.

Religion had become camouflage.

Jesus says in Matthew 23:

"Woe to you, scribes and Pharisees, hypocrites! For you clean the outside of the cup and the plate, but inside they are full of greed and self-indulgence" (Matt. 23:25, ESV).

What frightens me about that verse is how possible it is to look spiritually healthy externally while remaining internally unhealthy.

A person can:

- preach sermons,

- teach theology,

- lead ministries,

- defend doctrine,

- and maintain religious discipline,

while still remaining proud, emotionally disconnected, self-righteous, harsh, or spiritually exhausted underneath.

That possibility forces uncomfortable self-examination.

Because the truth is that survival-based Christianity naturally pushes people toward image management. When someone spends years trying to avoid shame, they often become deeply invested in appearing spiritually successful. They may unconsciously build identity around:

- being knowledgeable,

- being disciplined,

- being morally serious,

- being "right,"

- or being respected spiritually.

But eventually performance begins replacing intimacy with God.

That is what happened to the Pharisees.

Jesus tells them:

"This people honors me with their lips, but their heart is far from me" (Matt. 15:8, ESV).

That verse is terrifying because external religious behavior can coexist with internal distance from God.

A person can know theology and still not know Christ relationally.

I think that realization explains why Jesus often felt emotionally safer to broken people than religious communities did. The Pharisees approached sinners primarily through categories of contamination and moral evaluation. Jesus approached sinners through compassion and truth simultaneously.

That balance matters.

Jesus never minimized sin.
But He also never used truth to protect His superiority.

That is where many religious people fail.

Truth becomes a weapon instead of a doorway toward restoration.

I have seen this happen repeatedly inside church culture. People sometimes use doctrine defensively rather than redemptively. Theology becomes less about knowing God and more about protecting identity or proving spiritual seriousness.

And honestly, I have felt those instincts in myself too.

There is a subtle satisfaction that comes from feeling morally or theologically superior to others. The Pharisee in Luke 18 demonstrates this perfectly:

"God, I thank you that I am not like other men" (Luke 18:11, ESV).

That prayer sounds shocking out loud.
But I think many believers quietly think versions of it internally.

At least I know I have.

Maybe not verbally.
Maybe not consciously.
But spiritually.

It is easy to compare ourselves against visibly struggling people and feel secure by contrast. It is easy to use someone else's public failure to reassure ourselves about our own spiritual condition.

But Jesus completely dismantles that system.

The tax collector in Luke 18 simply prays:

"God, be merciful to me, a sinner!" (Luke 18:13, ESV).

And Jesus says the broken man went home justified instead.

Why?

Because humility creates space for grace.

The Pharisee remained trapped inside self-constructed righteousness. The tax collector brought truth into the light.

That difference still matters enormously.

I think one reason Jesus felt so threatening to religious leaders is because He exposed how much of their spirituality depended upon image, status, and performance. He kept dismantling the systems they used to reassure themselves.

He touched unclean people.
He defended social outcasts.
He ate with sinners.
He healed on the Sabbath.
He elevated humility over appearance repeatedly.

Every action threatened the religious illusion that righteousness could be measured externally.

And honestly, I think He still threatens that illusion today.

Because many believers still quietly build identity around:

- visible morality,

- doctrinal precision,

- church reputation,

- ministry involvement,

- and performance-based spirituality.

Meanwhile Jesus keeps asking about the heart.

Not the projected self.
The actual self.

The self beneath the camouflage.

That is deeply uncomfortable because truthful Christianity requires surrendering the image we carefully constructed for survival. It requires admitting weakness honestly. It requires acknowledging that no amount of religious performance can substitute for abiding in Christ.

Paul understood this eventually.

In Philippians 3, Paul lists his religious credentials:

- circumcised correctly,

- ethnically Jewish,

- a Pharisee,

- zealous,

- externally blameless regarding the law.

Then he says:

"Whatever gain I had, I counted as loss for the sake of Christ" (Phil. 3:7, ESV).

That is extraordinary.

Paul realized religious achievement itself could become an obstacle if it replaced dependence upon Christ.

And honestly, I think many of us need that realization too.

Because the greatest danger is not always rebellion against God.

Sometimes the greatest danger is building an identity so dependent upon appearing righteous that we never learn how to stand truthfully before Him instead.

The Pharisee in me wants certainty through performance.
Jesus keeps inviting me toward surrender instead.

Chapter "Six.Five"
The Strong Child Breaks

For most of my life, I thought strength meant carrying everything quietly.

Not complaining.

Not needing help.

Not becoming a burden.

Not letting people see weakness.

Not collapsing publicly.

I became hyper responsible long before I became healthy.

That is what many children from unstable environments learn to do. When chaos exists around you constantly, somebody has to become functional. Somebody has to stay alert. Somebody has to read the room, anticipate problems, manage emotions, avoid embarrassment, and keep moving forward no matter how exhausted they feel internally.

So you become "the strong one."

People praise you for it eventually.

You seem mature.

Responsible.

Competent.

Disciplined.

Calm under pressure.

But underneath that strength is often fear.

Fear that if you stop performing, everything falls apart.

I understand that now in ways I did not understand growing up.

As a child, I thought survival itself was maturity. I learned how to suppress emotion quickly because emotion did not solve instability. Hyper awareness felt safer than vulnerability. Competence felt safer than dependence.

Over time, that survival mindset quietly became identity.

Then adulthood reinforced it.

The military rewarded discipline, control, endurance, and carrying pressure without complaint. Emergency medicine rewarded calmness inside chaos. Law enforcement rewarded composure under stress, emotional restraint, and the ability to keep functioning while other people collapsed around you.

And honestly, I became very good at functioning.

Very good at carrying weight.
Very good at compartmentalizing pain.
Very good at continuing forward.

But functioning and healing are not the same thing.

That realization took me years to understand.

Because externally, competence can look incredibly similar to wholeness.

People praise strong people constantly while quietly ignoring whether those strong people are actually surviving internally. The strong child learns this quickly:
performance earns safety.

So the performance deepens.

You become dependable.
Capable.

Useful.

Helpful.

Respected.

Meanwhile the actual person underneath quietly disappears beneath responsibility.

The frightening thing is that eventually even you stop recognizing the difference between who you are and who you had to become in order to survive.

I think many men live this way.

Especially inside:

- military culture,

- law enforcement culture,

- EMS culture,

- and even church culture.

Men are often taught that emotional control equals maturity. Weakness becomes dangerous socially. Vulnerability threatens identity. So many men become emotionally armored while calling it strength.

But armor protects by limiting exposure.

And eventually armored people stop knowing how to rest.

I think that is one reason so many men secretly feel isolated even while functioning successfully outwardly. They know how to perform competence but not how to be known honestly. They know how to lead, provide, fix problems, and carry burdens, but they do not know how to confess weakness safely.

So they hide.

Some hide behind work.

Some behind theology.

Some behind ministry.

Some behind anger.

Some behind humor.

Some behind pornography.

Some behind achievement.

Some behind emotional distance.

But eventually the camouflage becomes exhausting.

I remember seasons where I felt emotionally and spiritually numb while still functioning outwardly. I could still work. Still lead. Still perform responsibilities. Still appear stable externally.

But internally something was cracking.

Exhaustion deepened.

Rest disappeared.

Prayer sometimes felt distant.

Church sometimes felt performative.

And honestly, I think part of me quietly feared what would happen if I stopped carrying everything myself.

Because carrying had become identity.

The strong child does not know how to collapse safely.

That sentence feels painfully true to me.

When you grow up believing weakness creates danger, collapse feels catastrophic. So you keep performing long past healthy limits. You continue functioning while internally deteriorating because functioning itself became survival.

But eventually performance reaches its limit.

Mine did.

There were seasons where life started stripping away the illusion that competence alone could save me. Losses accumulated. Exhaustion accumulated. Pressure accumulated. And underneath all of it sat a terrifying realization:
I could not carry myself forever.

I still find myself sitting alone in vehicles sometimes after long shifts without even turning them off immediately. Just sitting there in silence staring forward mentally exhausted in ways sleep does not really fix. Still functioning. Still carrying responsibility. Still appearing composed externally. But internally feeling disconnected from myself, from people, and sometimes even from God. Those moments frightened me because they revealed how long a person can survive outwardly while quietly collapsing inwardly.

That realization felt humiliating at first.

Because strong people often experience need as failure.

But slowly I began realizing something deeper:
Christianity was never asking me to carry myself independently in the first place.

Jesus says:

"Come to me, all who labor and are heavy laden, and I will give you rest" (Matt. 11:28, ESV).

I had quoted that verse for years.

But honestly, I often lived as though the real invitation was:

"Come perform."

"Come maintain yourself."

"Come prove your strength."

"Come hold everything together."

Meanwhile Christ kept offering rest instead.

Not passivity.

Not irresponsibility.

Dependence.

That word disturbed me deeply because dependence feels dangerous to people shaped by survival. Survival teaches self-protection. Self-management. Hyper vigilance. Independence.

The gospel teaches surrender.

And honestly, surrender felt harder than discipline ever did.

Discipline I understood.

Surrender required trust.

Trust that Christ would not abandon me if the performance stopped.

Trust that exposure would not destroy belonging.

Trust that weakness did not make me less valuable.

Trust that grace was real enough for exhausted people too.

That process changed how I began viewing Jesus entirely.

Because Jesus never seemed impressed by performative strength.

He moved toward weary people constantly.

Toward frightened people.

Toward collapsing people.

Toward exposed people.

Peter collapsed publicly.

Thomas doubted openly.

The disciples panicked repeatedly.

And Jesus kept moving toward them anyway.

That matters deeply because many strong people secretly believe love depends upon usefulness. They fear that if they stop functioning perfectly, they will lose value, belonging, or purpose.

But Christ consistently loved people before they proved anything.

That changes everything.

I think many believers are exhausted because they confuse strength with self-sufficiency. But biblical strength looks radically different from survival-based strength.

Paul writes:

"For when I am weak, then I am strong" (2 Cor. 12:10, ESV).

That verse makes no sense inside performance culture.

Weakness feels threatening there.

But in the kingdom of God, weakness becomes the place where dependence finally begins.

And honestly, I think that may be one reason Jesus felt different from every system built around image management and performance.

He did not merely tolerate exhausted people.

He invited them closer.

Not after they became stronger.
While they were weary.

The strong child in me spent years trying to carry everything quietly.

Christ kept teaching me something terrifying instead:

I was never supposed to carry myself alone.

PART III:
MISSING CHRIST

Chapter Seven:
Sabbath and Exhaustion

The Sabbath was supposed to teach rest.

That is what makes the exhaustion so tragic.

Somewhere along the way, many believers inherited a version of Christianity where even rest became work. Instead of experiencing Sabbath as delight, sanctuary, communion, and trust in God, people quietly learned how to experience it through anxiety.

Can I do this?
Should I do that?
Did I break the Sabbath?
Am I being worldly?
Am I acceptable to God right now?

What was designed as freedom slowly became surveillance.

I think many people inside Seventh-day Adventist Church know exactly what I mean even if they struggle to articulate it publicly. They grew up sincerely believing the Sabbath mattered deeply, and it does. I still believe that. But somewhere along the way, the beauty of Sabbath sometimes became buried beneath fear-based performance.

The day meant to reveal rest in God quietly became another test people were terrified of failing.

That realization disturbed me because when I looked at Jesus, He seemed to approach the Sabbath completely differently than many religious people around Him.

The Pharisees approached the Sabbath like border guards.
Jesus approached the Sabbath like restoration.

That distinction matters enormously.

In Mark 2, the Pharisees become angry because Jesus' disciples pluck grain while walking through the fields on the Sabbath. They immediately interpret the situation through violation categories. Their primary concern is technical compliance.

Jesus responds:

"The Sabbath was made for man, not man for the Sabbath" (Mark 2:27, ESV).

That statement changes everything.

The Sabbath was given as gift, not burden.
Restoration, not anxiety.
Relationship, not performance.

Yet religious people often transform gifts into measurements.

The Pharisees had become so focused on protecting the Sabbath externally that they lost sight of the God who created it originally. They guarded the institution while missing the heart behind it.

And honestly, I think we still do this constantly.

People become obsessed with behavioral precision while remaining emotionally exhausted, spiritually anxious, relationally disconnected, and inwardly terrified. Entire forms of Christianity quietly teach people that they are never fully doing enough.

Pray more.
Study more.
Perform better.
Be holier.
Appear stronger.
Hide weakness more effectively.

The result is often exhausted discipleship.

People know doctrine but not rest.
People know standards but not peace.

People know prophecy but not joy.

People know church culture but not intimacy with Christ.

That exhaustion reveals something important:
performance can imitate spirituality externally while slowly starving the soul internally.

Jesus confronted this repeatedly.

In Matthew 11, immediately before many of His Sabbath confrontations, Christ says:

"Come to me, all who labor and are heavy laden, and I will give you rest" (Matt. 11:28, ESV).

That invitation feels radically different from many religious systems.

Notice what Jesus does not say.

He does not say:
"Come prove yourself."
"Come impress Me."
"Come perfect your behavior first."

He says:
Come to Me.

That is relational language.

And honestly, I think many believers have spent years learning Christianity primarily through performance categories instead of relational categories. They ask:
Am I acceptable?
Am I failing?
Did I measure up?

Instead of:
Do I know Christ?
Am I abiding?
Am I surrendering honestly?

Those are very different spiritual frameworks.

One produces anxiety.
The other produces dependence.

The strange thing is that many deeply sincere Christians quietly live exhausted because they believe rest itself must somehow be earned. They know grace intellectually but function practically as though acceptance depends upon continual spiritual performance.

I understand that instinct well.

When someone grows up around instability, performance often becomes survival. If appearing correct keeps you safe socially, emotionally, or spiritually, then you naturally become hyper aware of behavior. You monitor yourself constantly. You fear mistakes. You fear exposure. You fear disappointing people or God.

Eventually spirituality itself can become exhausting because every moment feels evaluated.

That is not rest.

And honestly, I think this is one reason Jesus often clashed with religious leaders around the Sabbath specifically. The Sabbath exposed the deeper issue underneath Phariseeism:
they did not know how to stop performing.

Even rest became regulated performance.

Meanwhile Jesus healed people on the Sabbath constantly.

That matters.

He restored broken bodies on the very day religious leaders obsessed over technical compliance. Why? Because Jesus understood the Sabbath as restoration rather than restriction.

The Sabbath was always supposed to reveal something about God's character.

Not merely His authority.

His goodness.

His provision.

His trustworthiness.

His invitation into dependence.

In Genesis, God rests not because He is tired, but because creation is complete.
Sabbath begins from completion, not striving.

That is deeply theological.

The gospel works the same way.

Christ says on the cross:

"It is finished" (John 19:30, ESV).

Finished.

Yet many Christians continue living as though they must constantly complete what
Jesus already accomplished. They carry spiritual anxiety continually because
performance-based religion never allows people to feel secure.

There is always another expectation.
Another standard.
Another comparison.
Another hidden fear.

I think truthful Christianity probably looks quieter than many of us imagined. Less
performance. Less pretending. More confession. More humility. More listening. More
grace. More honesty about weakness. More room for exhausted people to breathe.
More churches where people do not have to disguise themselves in order to belong.
More believers who resemble Christ enough that wounded people feel safer moving
toward them instead of away from them. Not holiness without compassion. Not grace
without truth. But truthful discipleship shaped by the actual character of Jesus.

And honestly, I think many believers are exhausted not because Christianity is false, but because they inherited distorted forms of Christianity centered more around performance than presence.

That is why Jesus felt different.

Religious systems often said:
"Try harder."

Jesus said:
"Abide in Me."

Religious systems often created pressure.
Jesus created rest.

Not passivity.
Not compromise.
Not lawlessness.

Restful surrender.

That distinction matters deeply because many people secretly fear that if they stop striving constantly, they will become spiritually lazy or rebellious. But true rest in Christ does not produce indifference. It produces love, gratitude, humility, and transformed obedience flowing from relationship rather than fear.

Jesus says in John 15:

"Whoever abides in me and I in him, he it is that bears much fruit" (John 15:5, ESV).

Fruit grows from abiding.
Not from panic.

That realization slowly changed how I understood discipleship entirely.

Holiness is not frantic performance trying to secure acceptance.
Holiness is the fruit of remaining honestly connected to Christ.

The Sabbath was supposed to teach us that.

To stop striving.

To stop proving.

To stop carrying ourselves endlessly.

To trust God enough to rest.

But many people learned exhaustion instead.

And maybe that is one reason so many Christians secretly feel weary all the time.

They are trying to carry burdens Jesus never asked them to carry.

Chapter Eight
Truthful Christians

The longer I spent around church culture, the more I realized many Christians know how to appear truthful without actually being truthful.

That sounds harsh, but I do not mean people are always intentionally deceptive. Most are not. I think many believers are simply surviving inside systems where honesty feels dangerous. Over time, people adapt emotionally to the environment around them.

If weakness threatens belonging, people hide weakness.
If struggle threatens acceptance, people hide struggle.
If questions threaten reputation, people hide questions.

Eventually an entire culture of concealment develops while everyone continues calling it spiritual maturity.

That realization disturbed me deeply because Jesus consistently seemed to value truthfulness more than image.

Not polished truthfulness.
Not performative vulnerability.
Real truthfulness.

The kind where a person finally stops pretending before God.

One of the clearest examples appears in Luke 18. Jesus describes two men praying in the temple. One is a Pharisee. The other is a tax collector.

The Pharisee prays confidently:

"God, I thank you that I am not like other men" (Luke 18:11, ESV).

Then he lists his religious accomplishments.

The tax collector, meanwhile, stands far away unable even to lift his eyes toward heaven. He simply says:

"God, be merciful to me, a sinner!" (Luke 18:13, ESV).

Then Jesus says something absolutely devastating:

"This man went down to his house justified, rather than the other" (Luke 18:14, ESV).

That story reveals something deeply important:
God responds differently to truthful people than to performers.

The Pharisee sounded spiritually impressive.
The tax collector sounded desperate.

And desperation opened the door to grace.

I think many Christians secretly fear desperation because desperation exposes need. But Christianity actually begins there. Nobody comes to Christ through self-sufficiency. People come to Christ because eventually they realize they cannot save themselves.

The problem is that religious culture sometimes teaches people to conceal need rather than confess it.

So Christians become actors.

Some perform theological certainty.
Some perform emotional stability.
Some perform moral superiority.

Some perform spiritual strength.
Some perform ministry success.

Meanwhile the actual person underneath remains exhausted and unknown.

I understand that instinct because I lived inside it for years.

When you grow up learning survival, honesty can feel dangerous. You become skilled at presenting acceptable versions of yourself publicly. You monitor reactions carefully. You avoid exposing too much weakness because weakness historically created embarrassment, instability, rejection, or shame.

That mindset can easily become spiritualized.

People start treating Christianity like image management instead of surrender.

But Jesus continually disrupted image management.

He exposed hidden motives.
He confronted religious performance.
He forced people into truth.

Yet strangely, broken people usually felt safer around Him after exposure, not less safe.

That matters deeply.

In John 4, Jesus reveals the Samaritan woman's hidden life directly:

"You have had five husbands, and the one you now have is not your husband" (John 4:18, ESV).

What amazes me is that she does not run away permanently. Why? Because Jesus exposes her without dehumanizing her.

That distinction changes everything.

Religious performance often exposes people to reinforce superiority.
Jesus exposed people to restore them.

Those are radically different motivations.

One creates shame.
The other creates repentance and healing.

I think many churches struggle because they know how to preach truth doctrinally while failing to embody truthful grace relationally. People hear sermons about forgiveness while quietly feeling unsafe admitting weakness publicly.

So everyone keeps hiding.

Families hide dysfunction.
Leaders hide burnout.
Men hide addiction.
Women hide exhaustion.
Teenagers hide depression.
Churches hide conflict.

And eventually entire congregations become emotionally disconnected because nobody feels safe being fully known.

That is tragic because Scripture consistently connects healing with truthfulness.

James writes:

"Therefore, confess your sins to one another and pray for one another, that you may be healed" (James 5:16, ESV).

Healing requires exposure.

Not exposure for humiliation.

Exposure for restoration.

Churches often describe themselves as hospitals for sinners. But many wounded people quietly feel safer bleeding outside the building than inside it. In emergency medicine, healing begins when honesty becomes possible. Symptoms matter. Exposure matters. Accurate diagnosis matters. But many religious environments unintentionally teach people to hide wounds instead of uncovering them. People learn how to present edited versions of themselves rather than truthful ones. They offer acceptable weakness instead of actual confession. The tragedy is that hospitals cannot heal wounds people are terrified to uncover.

That is why camouflage Christianity becomes so spiritually destructive over time. A person cannot heal while continually protecting a false self. Eventually the performance itself becomes exhausting because maintaining image requires constant emotional energy.

David describes this after concealing sin:

"For when I kept silent, my bones wasted away through my groaning all day long" (Ps. 32:3, ESV).

Concealment corrodes people internally.

And honestly, many believers are carrying enormous internal exhaustion because they are trying to maintain identities they were never meant to sustain.

The gospel was never an invitation to construct a more convincing disguise. It was an invitation to die.

Jesus says:

"If anyone would come after me, let him deny himself and take up his cross daily and follow me" (Luke 9:23, ESV).

That includes the false self.
The performative self.
The camouflage self.

Truthful Christianity begins when people finally stop trying to save themselves through appearance.

That does not mean holiness disappears.
It means holiness finally becomes honest.

Not image centered holiness.
Christ centered holiness.

There is a massive difference.

Image centered holiness asks:
"How do I appear spiritually successful?"

Christ centered holiness asks:
"How do I abide honestly in Jesus?"

One produces anxiety.
The other produces surrender.

The strange thing is that many believers secretly fear truthful Christianity because they assume honesty will destroy belonging. But genuine Christian community cannot exist without truthfulness. Relationships built entirely around performance eventually become shallow because nobody is actually known.

John writes:

"But if we walk in the light, as he is in the light, we have fellowship with one another" (1 John 1:7, ESV).

Notice the connection.

Light produces fellowship.

Not performance.
Not camouflage.
Light.

That means true Christian community requires people willing to be seen honestly. Not perfectly. Honestly.

And honestly, I think that is one reason Jesus felt different from many religious systems. Around Jesus, people could stop pretending eventually. The masks became unnecessary because Christ already saw completely.

The woman at the well.
Peter after denial.
The sinful woman in Luke 7.
The tax collector in Luke 18.

They were all exposed already.

And somehow exposure became the beginning of restoration instead of the end of belonging.

I think many believers desperately need that realization.

Because some people have spent their entire lives trying to appear transformed while quietly remaining terrified of being truly known.

But Jesus never invited people into performance.

He invited them into truth.

Chapter Nine:
Why Jesus Felt Different

The older I became, the more I realized that what drew me toward Jesus was often the exact opposite of what exhausted me about religion.

Jesus felt different.

Not softer toward sin.
Not careless about truth.
Not indifferent toward holiness.

Different in the way He carried holiness.
Different in the way He approached broken people.
Different in the way people seemed to breathe around Him instead of perform around Him.

That distinction matters deeply.

Because many religious environments unintentionally teach people how to become spiritually tense. Everything feels monitored constantly:
behavior,

appearance,

language,

standards,

performance,

reputation.

People become hyper aware of themselves all the time.

But around Jesus, something strange kept happening.

Broken people moved toward Him instead of away from Him.

Rural Alaska changed the way I saw suffering. There are nights where silence settles so heavily over a village that you can feel the isolation physically. You respond to intoxication, violence, death notifications, broken homes, and generations of pain while people quietly carry exhaustion beneath visible survival. In some places there are no polished suburban facades hiding reality anymore. No carefully constructed appearances left to maintain. Just human beings trying to survive another winter, another loss, another night, another addiction, another funeral, another disappointment. In those moments, I began realizing how differently Jesus approached broken people compared to many religious systems. Christ moved toward exposed people. Many religious environments teach people to hide until they become acceptable first.

That should disturb religious people more than it usually does.

Tax collectors moved toward Him.
Prostitutes moved toward Him.
The ashamed moved toward Him.
The exhausted moved toward Him.
Sinners kept wanting to be near Him.

Meanwhile many religious leaders became angry, defensive, and threatened by Him.

That contrast says something profound.

In Luke 15, the Pharisees complain:

"This man receives sinners and eats with them" (Luke 15:2, ESV).

That sentence was intended as criticism.

But honestly, it may be one of the most beautiful descriptions of Jesus in the entire Gospels.

This man receives sinners.

Not tolerates them coldly.
Not merely lectures them.
Receives them.

That does not mean Jesus minimized sin. He absolutely confronted sin. But sinners somehow still felt safer near Jesus than near religious performers because Christ carried truth without superiority.

That difference changes everything.

Many forms of performance driven religion communicate:
"Clean yourself first, then come near."

Jesus says:
"Come near so transformation can begin."

Those are radically different spiritual environments.

I think many people secretly feel exhausted because they have spent years trying to achieve spiritual acceptability before allowing themselves to rest in God's presence. They assume they must first become spiritually impressive enough to deserve intimacy with Christ.

But the Gospel consistently reveals the opposite.

Jesus meets people in weakness constantly.

He meets Peter after failure.
Thomas inside doubt.
The Samaritan woman inside shame.
The demoniac inside chaos.
The thief on the cross-inside destruction.

Again and again, Jesus moves toward exposed people instead of away from them.

That mattered deeply to me because much of my early understanding of Christianity felt connected to concealment instead of rest. You learned how to avoid exposure. You learned how to appear spiritually acceptable. You learned how to survive church culture carefully.

But Jesus did not seem interested in carefully managed appearances.

In Matthew 11, He says:

"Come to me, all who labor and are heavy laden, and I will give you rest" (Matt. 11:28, ESV).

That invitation feels radically different from performative religion.

Religious performance says:
"Carry yourself."

Jesus says:
"Come rest."

Religious performance says:
"Become acceptable first."

Jesus says:
"Come near while weary."

Religious performance says:
"Hide weakness."

Jesus says:
"Bring your burdens."

That distinction slowly changed my understanding of Christianity entirely.

Because honestly, many believers are exhausted from carrying identities they were never meant to sustain. They are trying to maintain the appearance of transformation instead of remaining honestly connected to Christ.

And eventually performance becomes crushing.

I think that is why Jesus often spoke so strongly against the Pharisees. Not because He hated holiness, but because He hated the way religious performance distorted the character of God before wounded people.

The Pharisees frequently communicated:
God is difficult to approach.
God is disappointed.
God is watching for failure.
God is primarily concerned with technical correctness.

Meanwhile Jesus revealed:
God moves toward repentant sinners.
God restores failures.
God welcomes the weary.
God desires mercy alongside truth.

That is why Jesus says:

"Those who are well have no need of a physician, but those who are sick" (Matt. 9:12, ESV).

A physician moves toward sickness.

That sounds obvious until you realize many religious environments unintentionally move away from visible weakness instead. People become uncomfortable around struggling individuals because brokenness threatens the illusion of collective stability.

So churches quietly reward people who:

- appear composed,

- sound spiritually mature,

- avoid visible failure,

- and maintain respectable appearances.

Meanwhile hurting people often feel increasingly invisible.

But Jesus consistently saw invisible people.

The woman with the issue of blood.
Blind Bartimaeus.
Zacchaeus hiding in the tree.
The leper everyone avoided touching.
The sinful woman crying publicly.

Jesus noticed people religion often overlooked.

And honestly, I think that is one reason He felt emotionally safer than many religious systems.

Around Jesus, people could stop pretending eventually.

Not because sin stopped mattering.
Because grace became larger than performance.

That distinction transformed how I began understanding holiness itself.

Growing up, holiness sometimes felt connected primarily to separation from contamination. Holy people appeared distant from visible brokenness. They seemed controlled, polished, spiritually composed.

But Jesus demonstrated holiness differently.

His holiness moved toward contamination without becoming contaminated.

His holiness restored.

His holiness healed.

His holiness touched lepers.

His holiness defended ashamed people.

That means holiness is not fragility.

Jesus was not afraid of proximity to broken humanity.

And honestly, I think many Christians still struggle to believe that.

Some people genuinely believe God tolerates them reluctantly while remaining fundamentally disappointed in them. They know grace intellectually but emotionally live as though acceptance depends upon continual performance.

That creates exhaustion.

Because nobody can sustain perfection indefinitely.

Eventually the disguise cracks.

Eventually the hidden self surfaces.

Eventually people collapse under the weight of trying to carry themselves spiritually.

And maybe that collapse is not always destruction.

Maybe sometimes collapse becomes the beginning of truth.

Peter collapsed publicly after denying Christ three times. Yet after resurrection, Jesus does not destroy Peter. He restores him gently:

"Do you love me?" (John 21:17, ESV).

That question matters deeply.

Jesus did not begin with Peter's failure.

He began with relationship.

That is what makes Christianity fundamentally different from performance-based religion.

At the center of Christianity is not merely behavioral management.

At the center is Christ Himself.

Not simply:
"Behave correctly."
But:
"Follow Me."

Not:
"Perfect yourself."
But:
"Abide in Me."

That distinction may sound small, but honestly it changes everything.

Because many people learned religion before they learned relationship.
Performance before surrender.
Appearance before truth.
Adventism before Christ.

And maybe that is why Jesus still feels so different.

He is not asking people to construct better camouflage.

He is asking them to come out of hiding entirely.

PART FOUR:

BECOMING

REAHL

Interlude:
The Repossessed Car

I used to think collapse would look dramatic.

I imagined some visible breakdown where everything finally exploded publicly. I thought people would notice immediately. I thought collapse would announce itself clearly.

But honestly, collapse often happens quietly.

It happens while you are still functioning.

You still go to work.
Still answer calls.
Still show up.
Still wear the uniform.
Still smile.
Still pray publicly.
Still speak correctly.
Still appear stable enough that nobody asks questions.

Meanwhile something underneath you is slowly giving way.

That is how it happened for me.

There were seasons of my life where everything externally looked mostly functional while internally I felt hollow. Relationships strained. Financial pressure deepened. Exhaustion accumulated quietly. Prayer sometimes felt distant. Church sometimes felt performative. I could still function outwardly while internally feeling emotionally numb.

That is one of the frightening things about survival patterns:
people often praise you while you are quietly deteriorating.

Because performance hides collapse extremely well.

I remember the humiliation of losing things I thought stable people were supposed to keep. Losing a car feels small compared to death, addiction, violence, or catastrophe. But sometimes collapse reveals itself through ordinary losses that expose how fragile your internal world already was.

The repossession itself was not merely financial.

It felt symbolic.

Like life was stripping away the illusion that competence alone could save me.

For years I had built identity around functioning:
discipline,
responsibility,
performance,
carrying pressure,
remaining useful,
remaining composed.

But eventually usefulness becomes a cruel foundation for identity because human beings were never meant to carry themselves indefinitely.

And honestly, I do not think I realized how exhausted I truly was until things started falling apart.

That is the strange thing about high functioning people.
You can continue operating long after your soul has become tired.

Especially if your childhood taught you that weakness creates danger.

You keep moving.

Keep adapting.

Keep surviving.

Keep functioning.

The strong child becomes the competent adult.

Then the competent adult quietly becomes the exhausted adult.

Many men never learn how to collapse safely. They learn how to function. How to provide. How to endure. How to remain useful. Military culture reinforces it. Policing reinforces it. Emergency medicine reinforces it. Even church culture sometimes reinforces it by quietly rewarding stoicism more than honesty. So men become highly competent at carrying pressure while remaining emotionally disconnected from themselves. They survive through usefulness while quietly forgetting how to be known relationally.

I remember sitting alone at times feeling emotionally disconnected from myself, from people, and sometimes even from God. Not because I stopped believing. Honestly, I still believed theology deeply. I still believed truth mattered. I still believed Christ mattered.

But I think part of me had quietly confused Christianity with carrying myself successfully.

I knew how to strive.

I knew how to endure.

I knew how to survive pressure.

But I did not know how to rest honestly.

And eventually survival becomes exhausting because survival was never supposed to become identity permanently.

I think that is one reason Jesus' words began affecting me differently over time:

"Come to me, all who labor and are heavy laden, and I will give you rest" (Matt. 11:28, ESV).

I had read that verse countless times.

But during collapse, the verse stopped sounding decorative and started sounding necessary.

Because eventually there comes a moment where performance no longer works well enough to hide what is happening underneath.

The camouflage starts cracking.

And honestly, that terrified me.

Not because I feared failure financially.
Not because I feared embarrassment socially.

Because I feared exposure personally.

When you spend years building identity around competence, collapse feels like annihilation. The strong child does not know how to fail safely. Weakness feels dangerous. Need feels humiliating. Dependence feels terrifying.

So even during exhaustion, you keep trying to carry yourself.

But eventually something inside you realizes:
you cannot continue indefinitely.

I think that realization was one of the first truly honest moments of my spiritual life.

Not because I suddenly became spiritually mature.
Not because everything healed overnight.

But because I finally stopped pretending strength alone could save me.

And strangely, what I feared would destroy me became the place where grace finally started feeling real instead of theoretical.

Because when performance begins collapsing, something else becomes visible underneath it:
the actual person.

The frightened person.
The exhausted person.
The hidden person.
The person who spent years trying to remain acceptable.
The person terrified of becoming a burden.
The person who learned camouflage long before surrender.

And somehow Christ remained there.

Not disgusted.
Not impatient.
Not demanding stronger performance.

Present.

That realization changed me slowly.

Because for years I unconsciously lived as though the invitation of Christianity was:
"Come hold yourself together."

Meanwhile Jesus kept saying:
"Come to Me."

Not after perfection.

Not after stability.

Not after recovery.

While weary.

That distinction changes everything.

Looking back now, I think collapse stripped away illusions I did not even realize I was carrying. It exposed how much of my spirituality still depended upon usefulness, image management, and quiet self-preservation.

And honestly, maybe that is why collapse sometimes becomes mercy.

Because eventually the disguises stop working.

And once camouflage begins breaking apart, grace can finally reach the actual person underneath it.

Chapter Ten:
Collapse

I used to think collapse looked dramatic.

I imagined complete destruction.

Public breakdown.

Visible failure.

A moment where everything suddenly exploded at once.

But honestly, collapse often happens quietly.

It happens while you are still functioning.

You still go to work.

Still answer calls.

Still show up.

Still smile.

Still perform responsibilities.

Still wear the uniform.

Still speak correctly.

Still appear composed.

Meanwhile something underneath you is slowly giving way.

That is what happened to me.

For years, strength had become identity. I learned early that survival depended on usefulness, awareness, composure, and performance. So I became good at carrying weight quietly. Good at functioning under pressure. Good at compartmentalizing exhaustion.

The military reinforced it.

Emergency medicine reinforced it.

Law enforcement reinforced it.
Even church culture reinforced it.

Keep moving.
Stay composed.
Handle the mission.
Do not become the problem.

And honestly, I became very competent at surviving.

But eventually survival stops feeling like living.

I remember seasons where everything externally still looked mostly functional while internally I felt hollow. Prayer became harder. Rest disappeared. I felt emotionally numb at times while still operating professionally and spiritually outwardly.

There were nights after long shifts where I would sit alone inside the vehicle without turning it off immediately. Just staring forward in silence. The exhaustion did not feel physical anymore. It felt deeper than that. I was still functioning. Still responding. Still carrying responsibility. But internally I often felt emotionally detached from myself, from people, and sometimes even from God. That frightened me because it revealed how long a person can survive outwardly while quietly collapsing inwardly.

That is the strange thing about hidden exhaustion:
people often praise you while you are quietly deteriorating.

Because performance hides collapse well.

There were moments where losses started stacking together quietly.
Relationships strained.
Dreams shifted.

Identity cracked.

The pressure of constantly carrying myself became heavier and heavier.

And underneath all of it sat a terrifying realization:
I did not know who I was without performance.

That realization disturbed me deeply.

Because I had spent years building identity around:
competence,

discipline,

resilience,

and usefulness.

But usefulness is a dangerous foundation for identity because eventually every human being reaches limits.

And when strong people reach limits, they often experience shame instead of rest.

I remember seasons where I felt spiritually exhausted but did not fully know how to say it honestly. I knew theology. I knew doctrine. I knew how to explain Scripture. But internally I often felt like someone carrying enormous weight while pretending it was manageable.

Church sometimes made that harder.

Not intentionally always.
But many religious environments reward appearance more than honesty. People celebrate strength publicly while quietly avoiding weakness. So even exhausted believers learn how to camouflage themselves spiritually.

I did too.

I could still speak spiritually while feeling empty.

Still function while emotionally detached.

Still appear stable while internally unravelling.

And honestly, one of the most frightening realizations was this:

I no longer knew whether I was abiding in Christ or merely performing Christianity successfully.

That question haunted me.

Because performance can imitate spiritual maturity externally for a very long time.

You can:

- preach,

- serve,

- lead,

- defend theology,

- attend church,

- keep standards,

- and still quietly feel disconnected from rest.

Eventually I reached a point where I realized I could not continue carrying myself indefinitely.

I think that realization broke something in me.

Or maybe it finally exposed something.

Because underneath the competence and survival patterns was still the same frightened child trying desperately not to become a burden. Still trying to stay acceptable. Still trying to prove value through usefulness.

The strong child had simply learned adult forms of camouflage.

That realization was humiliating.

Not because I hated Christ.
Because I finally realized how much of my spirituality still depended upon self-preservation instead of surrender.

And honestly, surrender terrified me more than discipline ever did.

Discipline I understood.
Performance I understood.
Carrying weight I understood.

But dependence?
Rest?
Letting Christ hold what I could not?

That felt foreign.

I think many exhausted Christians secretly live there.

They know how to strive.
How to perform.
How to survive.
But they do not know how to collapse safely before God.

So they keep carrying themselves long past emotional and spiritual exhaustion.

But eventually performance stops working.

Mine did.

And strangely, what I feared would destroy me became the beginning of honesty instead.

Because collapse stripped away illusions.

It exposed how much of my identity had been built around usefulness instead of belovedness.
How much of my spirituality still functioned through fear.
How much energy I spent maintaining composure.
How deeply I feared weakness and exposure.

And underneath all of it, Christ remained there.

Not disgusted.
Not distant.
Not demanding stronger performance.

Present.

That realization changed me slowly.

Because for years I unconsciously believed God primarily wanted strength from me. Better discipline. Better consistency. Better spiritual performance.

Meanwhile Jesus kept saying:

"Come to me, all who labor and are heavy laden, and I will give you rest" (Matt. 11:28, ESV).

Rest.

Not because I finally became impressive enough.
But because I finally stopped pretending I could carry myself alone.

Looking back now, I think collapse may have been one of the first truly honest moments of my spiritual life.

Not because everything became fixed immediately.
Not because fear disappeared overnight.

But because camouflage finally started cracking.

And once camouflage cracks, grace can finally reach the actual person underneath it.

Chapter Eleven:
Exposure

I used to think exposure was the enemy.

Exposure meant danger.

Exposure meant embarrassment.

Exposure meant rejection.

Exposure meant people finally seeing what you spent years trying to conceal.

So I learned how to manage perception carefully.

Many people do.

Some manage perception through morality.

Some through intelligence.

Some through ministry.

Some through humor.

Some through achievement.

Some through theology.

Some through competence.

But underneath most performance is the same fear:

"If people truly knew me, would I still be loved?"

That fear shapes entire lives.

And honestly, I think many churches unknowingly reinforce it.

Not because every believer is cruel.

Not because nobody cares.

But because many religious environments quietly reward appearance.

People compliment strength.

Consistency.

Knowledge.

Discipline.

Leadership.

Composure.

Meanwhile weakness often becomes uncomfortable.

So people adapt.

They learn which struggles are acceptable to mention publicly and which ones must remain hidden. They learn how to confess "safe sins" while protecting deeper wounds carefully. They learn how to speak spiritually while remaining emotionally guarded.

And eventually many Christians become strangers to themselves.

I think that is one reason truthful confession feels so terrifying in church culture sometimes.

Because confession threatens the identity people worked years to construct.

Especially if survival taught them performance was necessary for safety.

That was true for me.

Honestly, part of me became very skilled at appearing spiritually grounded while remaining emotionally guarded. I could discuss theology while quietly avoiding vulnerability. I could help other people while struggling to admit my own exhaustion. I could preach surrender while still trying to manage my own image carefully. Sometimes usefulness felt safer than honesty because usefulness kept people from looking too closely at what was happening underneath.

I learned early how to monitor environments carefully. I learned how to appear functional even while chaos existed underneath the surface. I learned how to carry burdens privately. I learned how to remain useful. And over time usefulness quietly became part of identity itself.

So exposure felt catastrophic.

Not because I wanted rebellion.
Not because I hated truth.

Because I feared becoming unacceptable.

I think many believers quietly live there.

They still attend church.
Still believe doctrine.
Still defend theology.
Still participate outwardly.

Meanwhile internally they are terrified someone might finally see:

- the exhaustion,

- the numbness,

- the addiction,

- the loneliness,

- the anger,

- the fear,

- the doubts,

- the hidden grief,

- or the shame.

So they continue performing.

But eventually something becomes exhausting about carrying identities built entirely around concealment.

And honestly, I think that is why Jesus felt so dangerous to religious people.

Because Jesus exposed things.

Not merely behavior.
Motives.
Masks.
Hidden pride.
Hidden fear.
Hidden self-righteousness.

And strangely, the people most threatened by Jesus were often not the openly broken people.

It was the people most invested in maintaining image.

That still matters.

Because exposure threatens the false self.

The polished self.
The acceptable self.
The spiritually impressive self.
The controlled self.

And honestly, many of us quietly protect those versions of ourselves constantly.

But the false self cannot actually be healed.

Only the real person can be healed.

That realization changed how I began reading Scripture entirely.

Especially moments where Jesus interacted with exposed people.

The woman at the well had no ability to maintain religious image anymore. Her relationships already exposed her publicly. The sinful woman in Luke 7 entered a Pharisee's house already carrying visible shame. Everyone in the room already knew what kind of woman she was before she spoke. You can almost feel the tension in the silence. Simon watches her with disgust while she weeps openly at Jesus' feet. The Pharisee is busy measuring contamination while Jesus is receiving confession. One person sees a category. The other sees a human being collapsing honestly in front of Him. That difference explains so much about why exhausted people often moved toward Christ while religious performers felt threatened by Him. Peter openly failed. Thomas openly doubted. The demoniac among the tombs had already lost social acceptability completely.

And somehow Jesus consistently moved toward exposed people rather than away from them.

That difference matters deeply.

Because many people secretly assume:

"If God truly saw me fully, He would withdraw."

But Scripture repeatedly reveals the opposite.

Hebrews says:

"No creature is hidden from his sight" (Heb. 4:13, ESV).

For years that verse felt terrifying to me.

Now it feels freeing.

Because if Christ already sees fully, then camouflage becomes unnecessary.

Not holiness.
Camouflage.

That distinction matters enormously.

Exposure does not mean sin suddenly stops mattering. It means honesty becomes possible. Confession becomes possible. Healing becomes possible.

Because hidden things cannot be surrendered honestly.

And honestly, I think many Christians remain spiritually exhausted because they are trying to heal while still protecting the disguise.

But grace reaches truthfully surrendered people, not carefully managed personas.

And strangely, the more honestly I began bringing the hidden parts of myself before Christ, the more I realized He was not withdrawing from me. He remained present. Not excusing sin. Not ignoring truth. But staying near enough for healing to begin honestly.

That realization changed my understanding of repentance completely.

Repentance is not theatrical shame.
It is truthful surrender.

Not image management.
Not religious performance.
Not self-hatred.

Truth.

Bringing the real person before God instead of the projected self.

And honestly, I think that is why truthful Christianity feels so rare sometimes.

Truthful Christianity requires exposure.

Not performative vulnerability.
Not curated authenticity.

Real honesty.

The kind that risks being seen fully.

And that is terrifying for people who survived through concealment.

But maybe exposure is not destruction after all.

Maybe exposure is the first place where grace finally reaches the actual person underneath the camouflage.

Because Christ never asked us to become invisible behind performance.

He asked us to come into the light.

And remain there with Him without pretending anymore.

Chapter Twelve: Abiding

For most of my life, I thought spiritual growth primarily meant becoming better at managing myself.

Better discipline.

Better behavior.

Better control.

Better performance.

Better appearance.

Even when grace was preached intellectually, I often interpreted Christianity practically through effort. I assumed maturity meant learning how to maintain the Christian life successfully through increasing spiritual performance.

But eventually that framework becomes exhausting.

Because no matter how disciplined a person becomes, the hidden self never fully disappears through behavior management alone. Fear remains. Pride remains. Shame remains. Loneliness remains. Exhaustion remains. A person can improve external habits while still remaining internally disconnected from rest, joy, intimacy with God, or truthful self-awareness.

That realization slowly forced me back toward Jesus' words themselves.

Again and again, Christ kept describing spiritual life relationally instead of performatively.

Not:

Manage yourself.

Impress Me.

Construct righteousness.

But:

"Abide in me, and I in you" (John 15:4, ESV).

That word changed everything for me eventually.

Abide.

Remain.
Stay connected.
Rest relationally.
Depend continuously.

Jesus did not describe the Christian life primarily as self-construction. He described it as attachment.

That is profoundly different.

Especially for people who grew up surviving through self-protection and performance.

Survival teaches independence.
The gospel teaches dependence.

Survival teaches concealment.
The gospel teaches surrender.

Survival teaches image management.
The gospel teaches abiding.

Those systems constantly collide inside people.

I remember realizing at one point that I spent more energy monitoring myself spiritually than actually resting in Christ. Even prayer could quietly become another performance metric. I could evaluate myself constantly while remaining emotionally disconnected from peace.

I think many believers genuinely love Christ while still functioning emotionally through survival patterns learned years earlier. They continue carrying themselves spiritually because they do not fully trust what happens if they stop performing.

Honestly, I understand that fear deeply.

Performance at least creates the illusion of control. If spirituality depends primarily upon my effort, my discipline, my theological precision, or my behavior, then at least I can measure progress visibly. But abiding feels different because abiding requires trust.

Trust that Christ is sufficient.
Trust that grace is real.
Trust that exposure will not destroy belonging.
Trust that surrender matters more than performance.

That kind of trust feels terrifying to people accustomed to camouflage.

Yet Jesus continually invites people there anyway.

In John 15, Christ says:

"Whoever abides in me and I in him, he it is that bears much fruit, for apart from me you can do nothing" (John 15:5, ESV).

That verse destroys performance-based Christianity completely.

Apart from Me you can do nothing.

Not:

"Apart from enough effort."

"Apart from stronger discipline."

"Apart from better image management."

Apart from Me.

The Christian life was never designed to function independently from continual relationship with Christ. But many believers quietly attempt exactly that. They try to sustain spirituality through religious systems, intellectual knowledge, moral effort, or public appearance while remaining emotionally disconnected from Jesus Himself.

The result is often spiritual exhaustion.

People know theology but not peace.
Doctrine but not intimacy.
Standards but not rest.
Church culture but not joy.

And eventually many begin wondering why Christianity feels so heavy all the time.

I think part of the answer is simple:

they are trying to carry what only abiding can sustain.

Fruit does not strain itself into existence.

Branches do not scream themselves into producing grapes.

Fruit grows naturally through connection.

That image matters deeply because many Christians quietly live as though sanctification happens primarily through panic, fear, and relentless self-monitoring.

But Jesus describes something much more relational.

Abide in Me.

Not passive Christianity.
Not careless Christianity.
Connected Christianity.

This realization also changed how I understood obedience.

Growing up, obedience sometimes felt disconnected from relationship. Rules existed almost independently from intimacy with God. The focus often became compliance itself rather than communion with Christ.

But Jesus says:

"If you love me, you will keep my commandments" (John 14:15, ESV).

Love precedes obedience.

That order matters enormously.

When obedience becomes disconnected from relationship, Christianity slowly transforms into behavioral anxiety. People constantly monitor themselves trying to secure reassurance through performance. But when obedience flows from abiding, holiness becomes relational instead of performative.

Not:

"Behave so God accepts you."

But:

"Remain connected to Christ and let Him transform you."

That difference changes everything internally.

Because abiding creates humility.

The branch cannot boast about fruit independently. Everything comes from connection to the vine. That destroys spiritual superiority because genuine transformation becomes impossible apart from grace.

I think this is one reason Jesus felt different from many religious systems.

Religious systems often create pressure centered around performance:

try harder,
be better,
appear stronger,
measure up.

Jesus creates dependence.

And honestly, dependence offends pride.

People want formulas.
Control.
Measurements.
Visible reassurance.

But abiding requires surrendering self-sufficiency entirely.

That is difficult for survival-oriented people especially because survival often depends upon hyper vigilance and self-management. Relaxing into dependence can feel unsafe emotionally.

In military environments, policing, and emergency medicine, composure becomes survival. You learn quickly to stay alert, stay functional, and keep moving under pressure. But spiritually, that same survival mentality can quietly make intimacy with God difficult because abiding requires surrender instead of control.

Yet Jesus repeatedly invites exhausted people into exactly that kind of rest:

"Come to me, all who labor and are heavy laden, and I will give you rest" (Matt. 11:28, ESV).

Rest.

Not merely future rest in heaven.

Present rest in relationship with Him.

That realization slowly changed how I viewed spiritual maturity entirely.

Spiritual maturity is not merely becoming more polished externally.

It is becoming more dependent internally.

More truthful.
More surrendered.
Humbler.
More connected to Christ.

Ironically, truly mature Christians often appear less performative, not more. They become less interested in image management because their identity increasingly rests in Christ rather than public perception.

That does not produce laziness.

It produces freedom.

Freedom to confess.

Freedom to repent.

Freedom to stop pretending constantly.

Freedom to let grace reach hidden places previously protected by camouflage.

I think many Christians fear this kind of surrender because they assume if they stop striving constantly, they will drift spiritually. But abiding is not spiritual passivity.

Abiding is active dependence.

It is waking up daily aware:

I cannot carry myself.

I cannot transform myself.

I cannot manufacture righteousness independently.

I need Christ continually.

That realization may actually be the beginning of truthful Christianity.

Not the destruction of holiness.

The restoration of it.

Because holiness separated from abiding eventually becomes performance.

But holiness flowing from abiding becomes the natural fruit of remaining close to Jesus Himself.

Maybe abiding is finally putting down the weight you spent years convincing yourself you had to carry alone.

And honestly, maybe that is what many believers were searching for all along without realizing it.

Not another system.

Not more camouflage.

Not better performance.

Just Christ.

Chapter Thirteen: Stop Hiding

I think many people are tired.

Not physically tired only.

Soul tired.

Tired from carrying versions of themselves they were never meant to sustain.
Tired from trying to appear spiritually stable while quietly unravelling internally.
Tired from monitoring behavior constantly.
Tired from performing strength.
Tired from pretending transformation while secretly feeling disconnected from God.

And honestly, I understand that exhaustion deeply.

Because survival teaches people how to hide long before it teaches them how to rest.

Some people learn to hide behind success.
Some behind humor.
Some behind theology.
Some behind ministry.
Some behind discipline.
Some behind busyness.
Some behind morality.

But eventually the camouflage becomes unbearable.

That is one of the deepest tragedies of performative Christianity:
people spend so much time constructing acceptable versions of themselves that
they lose touch with the actual person Christ wants to heal.

The frightened person.
The ashamed person.
The exhausted person.
The lonely person.
The angry person.
The addicted person.
The performative person.

The real person.

And honestly, I think that is why Jesus' invitations feel so radically different from religious performance systems.

Jesus never said:

"Perfect yourself first."
"Construct a convincing disguise."
"Become impressive enough for Me."

He said:

"Come to me" (Matt. 11:28, ESV).

That invitation sounds simple until you realize how terrifying it becomes for people accustomed to hiding.

Because coming to Christ honestly eventually requires surrendering camouflage.

Not pretending.
Not managing image.
Not selectively presenting acceptable pieces of yourself.

Truth.

And truth feels dangerous to people who survived through concealment.

I think that is why many believers quietly stay exhausted for years. They know theology intellectually while remaining emotionally disconnected from grace. They understand doctrine while still functioning internally through fear, shame, performance, and self-protection.

They learned Christianity culturally before they learned surrender relationally.

I understand that because much of my own life was shaped by trying to survive instability while appearing normal externally. I learned how to monitor environments carefully. I learned how to avoid exposure. I learned how to present acceptable versions of myself publicly while quietly carrying fear and exhaustion privately.

Church sometimes reinforced those instincts unintentionally.

Not because everyone was malicious.

But because religious cultures often reward appearance naturally.

Many people are not afraid of Christ Himself. They are afraid of exposure without grace. Afraid of becoming prayer requests instead of people. Afraid of gossip disguised as concern. Afraid of conditional belonging that disappears the moment weakness becomes visible. Afraid of being treated like projects instead of human beings. In some church environments, people quietly learn that honesty can cost them reputation, leadership, relationships, or acceptance. So they adapt. They become careful. Measured. Filtered. Eventually they stop confessing altogether and simply learn how to perform spiritual stability publicly while suffering privately.

Churches often describe themselves as hospitals for sinners. But many wounded people quietly feel safer bleeding outside the building than inside it. In emergency medicine, healing begins when honesty becomes possible. Symptoms matter. Exposure matters. Accurate diagnosis matters. But many religious environments unintentionally teach people to hide wounds instead of uncovering them. People learn how to present edited versions of themselves rather than truthful ones. They offer acceptable weakness instead of actual confession. They learn how to survive spiritually while remaining emotionally hidden. The tragedy is that hospitals cannot heal wounds people are terrified to uncover.

People praise strength.
Competence.
Discipline.
Spiritual confidence.

Meanwhile weakness becomes uncomfortable.

So people continue hiding.

The terrifying thing is that eventually hiding starts feeling normal.

A person can spend years:
attending church,
defending doctrine,
participating in ministry,
keeping standards,
and appearing spiritually mature,

while quietly remaining disconnected from truthful intimacy with Christ.

That realization disturbed me deeply because Jesus constantly seemed to move in the opposite direction.

He kept drawing hidden things into the light.

Not to destroy people.

To free them.

The woman at the well.
The sinful woman in Luke 7.
Peter after denial.
Thomas inside doubt.
The demoniac among the tombs.

Again and again, Jesus met people exactly where camouflage finally failed.

And strangely, those moments of exposure often became the beginning of transformation rather than the end of belonging.

That matters enormously.

Because many believers still assume:

"If people truly knew me, I would be rejected."

But the gospel reveals something radically different:

Christ already knows fully.

Hebrews says:

"No creature is hidden from his sight" (Heb. 4:13, ESV).

That verse used to feel terrifying to me.

Now it feels freeing.

Because if Christ already sees completely, then the exhausting burden of maintaining disguise becomes unnecessary. The false self no longer needs protection constantly.

That does not mean sin becomes irrelevant.

It means hiding becomes unnecessary.

There is a massive difference.

Truthful Christianity is not the abandonment of holiness.

It is the abandonment of performance as identity.

That distinction matters deeply because many people secretly confuse the two.

Some hear criticism of performative religion and assume the answer must be compromise, lawlessness, or theological carelessness. But that is not what I am arguing at all.

I still believe truth matters.
I still believe obedience matters.
I still believe the law of God matters.
I still believe the Sabbath matters.
I still believe theology matters deeply.

But I also believe many people learned systems before they learned surrender.

And systems without Christ eventually become exhausting.

That is why Jesus felt different.

He was truthful without cruelty.
Holy without superiority.
Strong without performance.
Compassionate without compromise.

He exposed sin while still moving toward sinners.

That combination changes everything.

Because people no longer need to choose between truth and grace in Christ. He embodies both perfectly.

John writes:

"And the Word became flesh and dwelt among us... full of grace and truth" (John 1:14, ESV).

Both.

Not grace without truth.
Not truth without grace.

Grace and truth together.

I think many churches unintentionally emphasize one while neglecting the other. Some emphasize truth until wounded people feel unsafe being honest. Others emphasize acceptance until transformation disappears entirely.

Jesus carried both perfectly.

And honestly, that is what many exhausted believers are actually searching for.

Not easier religion.
Not watered-down theology.
Not permission to stay unchanged.

They are searching for truthful Christianity.

Christianity where:

- confession exists,

- grace is real,

- holiness remains relational,

- weakness can be acknowledged,

- hiddenness loses power,

- and Christ stands at the center instead of performance.

Because eventually every disguise crack.

The strong child collapses eventually.
The polished believer collapses eventually.
The performer collapses eventually.

And maybe that collapse is not the end.

Maybe it is the beginning of finally becoming truthful before God.

Some parts of us never formed cleanly. Some identities were built in survival instead of safety. Some stories remained interrupted beneath outward functionality for years. Maybe that is why this book contains a "half chapter." Because many people themselves feel unfinished internally. Fragmented. Hidden somewhere between survival and surrender, between performance and truth, between the border guard and the Pharisee.

Maybe the thing many of us feared most, being fully seen, becomes the very place where grace finally reaches us honestly for the first time.

I think that is the invitation Jesus has always been offering.

Not:

"Hide better."

But:

"Come into the light."

Not:

"Construct a stronger image."

But:

"Abide in Me."

Not:

"Perform transformation."

But:

"Surrender honestly."

Because Christianity was never supposed to be camouflage.

It was never meant to train people to disappear behind religious language.

It was always supposed to be Christ.

Conclusion:
The Bicycle in Plain Sight

I think about the border guard story often.

A man crosses the border every day carrying bags of sand on a bicycle. The officer becomes obsessed with the sand. He searches it constantly, convinced something hidden must be there. He spends years focused on details, patterns, and technicalities while the obvious thing passes directly in front of him over and over again.

The man was smuggling bicycles.

The story stays with me because it feels painfully familiar.

I think many of us spent years sifting religious sand while quietly missing Christ standing in plain sight.

Not because truth did not matter.
Not because doctrine was meaningless.

But because human beings naturally drift toward systems, measurements, and performance. Rules feel safer than surrender. Appearances feel safer than exposure. Technical correctness feels easier to control than relational dependence.

So people learn religion.

Sometimes before they learn Christ.

That realization became impossible for me to ignore as I grew older. I started seeing how many believers quietly lived exhausted lives beneath polished spiritual appearances. People knew how to:

- behave correctly,

- speak spiritually,

- defend doctrine,

- participate in church culture,

- and maintain religious image,

while privately carrying fear, shame, loneliness, addiction, bitterness, confusion, or emotional exhaustion underneath.

And honestly, I understood them because I had lived inside those same survival systems myself.

I knew what it meant to hide.
To monitor appearances.
To protect the camouflage carefully.
To fear exposure.
To confuse performance with transformation.

But eventually camouflage becomes exhausting.

Eventually the soul becomes tired from carrying identities built around concealment instead of truth.

That exhaustion matters because I think many Christians secretly believe they are failing spiritually when in reality they are simply carrying burdens Christ never asked them to carry.

Jesus never said:

"Carry yourself endlessly."

He said:

"Come to me, all who labor and are heavy laden, and I will give you rest" (Matt. 11:28, ESV).

Rest.

That word feels almost foreign inside many religious environments because people quietly learn how to strive spiritually instead. They monitor themselves constantly. They fear mistakes constantly. They compare themselves constantly. They try to maintain acceptable appearances constantly.

But Jesus continually invited people into something radically different:

abiding.

Not performance.
Relationship.

Not camouflage.
Truth.

Not image management.
Surrender.

That distinction changes everything.

Because Christianity was never ultimately about constructing a convincing religious identity. It was always about Christ Himself.

Not merely knowing about Him.
Knowing Him.

Not merely defending theology.
Abiding relationally.

Not merely preserving systems.
Becoming transformed through grace.

That realization does not make doctrine irrelevant. If anything, it makes doctrine more beautiful because theology finally becomes connected to the actual character of Christ instead of functioning merely as religious information.

The Sabbath becomes rest again.
Grace becomes real again.
Confession becomes healing again.
Holiness becomes relational again.
Truth becomes restorative again.

And honestly, maybe that is what many believers were searching for the entire time without fully realizing it.

Not easier Christianity.
Not compromise.
Not permission to remain unchanged.

Just truthful Christianity.

Christianity where people no longer need to pretend they are already healed in order to belong.
Christianity where grace reaches hidden places.
Christianity where confession is not social suicide.
Christianity where theology leads toward Christ instead of away from Him.
Christianity where broken people can stop hiding long enough to be loved honestly.

Because eventually everyone reaches the same question.

Who am I underneath the camouflage?

Not the projected self.
Not the church version.

Not the polished version.

Not the survival version.

The real person.

And the gospel answers that question differently than performance-based religion does.

Performance says:

"Hide weakness until you become acceptable."

Jesus says:

"Bring your weakness into the light so transformation can begin."

That difference may be the entire point.

The woman at the well.
The tax collector.
Peter after denial.
The sinful woman in Luke 7.
Thomas inside doubt.

Again and again, Jesus met exposed people with truth and grace simultaneously.

Not minimizing sin.
Not celebrating brokenness.

But refusing to abandon broken people because of it.

That is why Jesus still feels different from religion centered around image management.

He does not ask for camouflage.

He asks for surrender.

And honestly, I think many believers are exhausted because they spent years learning how to perform Christianity before learning how to abide in Christ.

The strong child collapses eventually.
The polished believer collapses eventually.
The performer collapses eventually.

And maybe that collapse is not the end.

Maybe it is the beginning of finally becoming truthful before God.

Some parts of us never formed cleanly. Some identities were built in survival instead of safety. Some stories remained interrupted beneath outward functionality for years. Maybe that is why this book contains a "half chapter." Because many people themselves feel unfinished internally. Fragmented. Hidden somewhere between survival and surrender, between performance and truth, between the border guard and the Pharisee.

Maybe the thing many of us feared most, being fully seen, becomes the very place where grace finally reaches us honestly for the first time.

I think that is the invitation Jesus has always been offering.

Not:
"Hide better."

But:
"Come into the light."

Not:
"Construct a stronger image."

But:
"Abide in Me."

Not:

"Perform transformation."

But:

"Surrender honestly."

Because Christianity was never supposed to be camouflage.

It was always supposed to be Christ.

And maybe that is why the bicycle matters so much.

Because the obvious thing was there the entire time.

Christ.
His grace.
His invitation.
His rest.
His presence.
His righteousness.
His call to truthful surrender.

Standing directly in front of us while we inspected sand.

This book is not really about rejecting Seventh-day Adventist Church.

It is about refusing to let systems replace the Savior.

It is about rediscovering the Christ many people quietly lost beneath performance, fear, shame, and camouflage.

It is about learning that holiness without love becomes distortion.
Truth without grace becomes brutality.
Religion without Christ becomes exhaustion.

And maybe most importantly, it is about finally understanding that the invitation of Jesus has never changed.

Not:

"Perfect yourself."

Not:

"Construct a stronger disguise."

Not:

"Become impressive enough."

Simply:

"Follow me" (Matt. 4:19, ESV).

For some people, that may begin with theology.

For others, it may begin with collapse.

For many of us, it begins the moment we finally stop hiding.